ON OUR WAY REJOICING

David J. Hetland

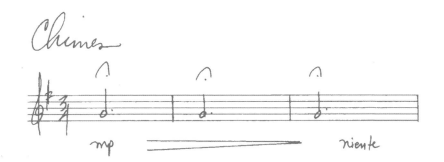

Recollections from the Concordia College Christmas Concerts

ON OUR WAY REJOICING

Recollections from the Concordia College Christmas Concerts
By DAVID J. HETLAND

Published by
Concordia College
901 South Eighth Street
Moorhead, Minnesota 56562

*This book is gratefully dedicated to
the founders and all participants of the
Concordia College Christmas Concerts,
to the lasting memory of
Paul J. Christiansen and Cyrus M. Running
and to Mary and Kristen for
their love and support.*

ISBN 0-9630111-3-8

Printed and bound in Canada by
Friesens Printers, Altona, Manitoba

To order additional copies of *On Our Way Rejoicing,*
dial toll-free **1-800-828-6409,** or visit our web site at
www.concordiarecordings.com

Paul J. Christiansen and Cyrus M. Running began their long collaboration on the Concordia College Christmas Concerts in 1940.

Front cover background: René Clausen conducted the massed Concordia choirs in 1997's concert, "Let Heaven and Nature Sing." *Insets:* Cy Running and Paul Christiansen conferred on Christmas Concert art and texts; David Hetland applied the finishing touches to the central image of the 1996 mural; television brought the dramatically lighted concerts to a nationwide audience in 1997.

TABLE OF CONTENTS

BEHOLD I MAKE ALL THINGS NEW

1990 Concordia College Christmas Concert

FOREWORD

For the large and faithful flock of Christmas Concert goers, *On Our Way Rejoicing*—a history of the Concordia Christmas Concert tradition—will spark powerful memories, please your eye and tempt your ear. And for those uninitiated in the tradition, this book will inspire you with stories of vision and excellence and, in all likelihood, will draw you into active involvement.

I attended my first Christmas Concert in 1952 in what was then the new Concordia Memorial Auditorium. For the first time, this concert had a facility suited to its needs and possibilities. There was plenty of room for art, choirs, instrumentalists, Christmas trees, special lighting effects and for people—as many as 6,000 per concert. For a 17-year-old college freshman, it was a spine-tingling, awe-inspiring introduction to the tradition. And my story has been repeated in the lives of thousands of people over the nearly 75 years of this concert.

I have been referring to this annual event as a concert only because it is the convention of the culture to call it by that name. It certainly is an artistic experience and, therefore, deserves to be called a concert. But, in fact, it is a good deal more than that. The synchronism of word, music and visual art makes it a liturgical experience. And the impact of these elements creates a religious experience for the listener.

Concordia College is pleased to sponsor this annual event for many reasons. First and foremost, it is a spiritual gift to the community. In addition, the concert is an expression of the college's mission and character; it illustrates the excellence to which we aspire. And the concert provides a wonderful homecoming for kindred spirits.

This book has been a long time in coming, and its publication would not have occurred without the vision, dedication and art of David Hetland. While there is not much of David in this story, let the record note that he has been coordinating visual art for this concert since 1978. It is fitting that David has prepared this book, for his engagement in this venture has been a matter of heart and soul, and his primary mentors in this tradition, Cyrus M. Running and Paul J. Christiansen, recognized early on his genius in these matters. And so, too, will you, the reader.

Finally, I wish to salute the lives and work of Clara Duea, Herman Monson, Paul Christiansen, Cy Running, David Hetland and René Clausen, who have guided and shaped this profound tradition. In each case their service was, or is, motivated not for the purpose of self-adulation, but for the glory of God.

Soli Deo Gloria

Paul J. Dovre
Concordia College President 1975-1999

INTRODUCTION

David Hetland studied with Cyrus Running and collaborated on these 1969 church mosaic panels and many Concordia Christmas Concerts.

For more than half of my life, I have helped prepare the annual Concordia College Christmas Concert—first as a student painter and later as its mural designer. To call this my most important project of each year would be an understatement. The truth is that I love this event, and it has been my privilege to know and work with so many of its talented personalities, past and present.

You, too, will meet them here—on a journey spanning nearly 75 years as they helped give shape to this very significant and colorful event. You will be introduced to the marvel and diversity of their unique talents, the selfless generosity of their combined spirit and the enduring legacy of their Christian service.

My fascination with Concordia's "Christmas gift to the Midwest" began when I caught my first glimpse of a Cyrus Running Christmas mural as a college freshman in 1965. Two years later, Mr. Running asked me to head the student art committee—to recruit painters and provide general project supervision. It would be a life-changing appointment, one that would ultimately lead me to a career in liturgical art. My debt to him remains enormous, and I am convinced that he yet helps to guide my hand and my heart.

Soon after my Christmas Concert association began, I became committed to gathering as much of the diverse concert memorabilia—photographs, program covers, original mural designs, clippings and anecdotes —as I could find. This volume features much of that collection plus a virtual mountain of material generously contributed by alumni and other friends of the college. More than enough was assembled to have easily made this book two or three times larger. Time and budget constraints, however, have demanded a reluctantly ruthless editing process, and I apologize to those whose material necessarily wound up on the cutting room floor. Perhaps, one day, there will be an expanded revision.

But, for now, this book is packed with treasured stories and images, arranged to parallel the structure of the concerts themselves. Beginning with the *prelude* of predecessor and parallel events, the story continues with sections featuring the word, music, art, production, outreach and legacy or *compline*. Whether or not readers have had a previous connection to Concordia College, my hope is that they will discover lasting and poignant insight mixed among occasional touches of wit and whimsy.

Now and then, my voice will be heard describing people or events. For the sake of continuity, I tried very hard to write these pages in a more objective, third-person style, but sometimes, I just couldn't help myself. As long-time Concordia administrator J.L. Rendahl would often say, "I'm not a historian—I was there." So I hope that you'll pardon my occasional intrusion.

In the midst of my research for this project, a coincidental discovery was made in the basement of Concordia's music hall. It was a collection of lectures written a half-century ago by F. Melius Christiansen, widely recognized as the "father of American choral music"—and the father of Paul J. Christiansen, who brought lasting structure to the Concordia Christmas Concerts.

In one of the elder Christiansen's treatises, simply titled "Choir Work," he wrote, "Nature takes a whole year to produce a flower. It is necessary to work many years to produce an artist. Any artistic production is the result of long and patient preparation." What an apt analogy for the Christmas Concert and its many participants, who bring to the event a lifetime of dedicated preparation—regardless of their roles. And so, this flower continues to bloom.

Christmas at Concordia has always been a time for the college to extend its embracing arms to members of its own family and to the community at large. May these pages do likewise, by bringing to you

Christmas blessings—every day.

David J. Hetland

During Concordia's first half century, students, faculty, staff members and their families looked forward to the Christmas Tree Parties held in the college gymnasium just before Christmas vacation.

"Ah! What a sight, and what feeling to sit there in the twilight and look at the glory and listen to the sounds!"

—Concordia *Crescent*, 1919 on the Christmas Tree Party

Chapter 1

PRELUDE: IN THE BEGINNING

Predecessor and Parallel Events

*any of the students who came from small towns and rural parishes to attend Concordia College in Moorhead, Minnesota, had spoken Norwegian before they learned English. They were eager to learn but homesick – and for them, **this** was the beginning of Christmas.*

In the darkness of the high-ceilinged gymnasium (one day to become the "art barn"), students gathered with teachers and their families, each carrying a small gift to place under the tree. Brightly lit, the Christmas tree illuminated the old gym and the upturned faces as they sang the familiar carols – English and, especially, Norwegian – they'd all loved as children.

In Concordia's first years, this traditional "Christmas Tree Party" provided the annual holiday celebration for the whole college—students, faculty members and their children. Celebrated on the last evening before Christmas vacation began, the program typically featured music provided, in various early years, by a choir, band, piano and vocal soloists and even (in 1920) the "Mondamin orchestra." Following the music was a short address by college president J.A. Aasgaard. And then everyone joined hands and marched around and around the Christmas tree, singing "the dear and beautiful Christmas songs," according to the 1919 college newspaper, *The Crescent.* "This event has been an annual custom here at Concordia, and besides being a means of showing that Christmas has come, it has served to create a feeling that we belong to one family," reported *The Concordian* in 1920.

In these early celebrations—annual events of music and light, heralding the coming of Christmas—it is easy to trace the roots of what eventually became the harmony of song and image that grace the renowned Concordia Christmas Concerts.

CAROLING AROUND THE TREE

During the first 50 years of the college, the Christmas Tree Parties were a tradition not to be missed, the last all-college event before the holiday break. Mildred (Knudsvig) Wermager '32*, who would later sing in the choir, was a 14-year-old visiting her sister at Concordia in 1924: "I recall the joy and excitement of having college girls curl my hair and find a *sleeveless* party dress for me to wear. It was an exciting evening for me, as other students seemed to think it was fun to give this shy little girl a good time."

A tall evergreen adorned the center of the gymnasium floor at the party, usually sponsored by the junior class. Some years, a play was performed first; in 1919 it was something called "Mrs. Tubbs Does Her Bit," presented by the Periclesian and Delphic Oracle literary societies. In the gym, the tree awaited. There was music; sometimes the young children of faculty members delivered songs or recitations.

At the end of the evening all exchanged gifts and treats: apples, candy, popcorn balls and peanuts. Gift exchanges provided "a great deal of merriment," according to *The*

Crescent. Gifts were not to exceed 10 or 15 cents in cost, and students enjoyed showing the curious choices, from Kewpie dolls to tiny threshing machines. By 1923, so many took part that the party committee

Caroling around the tree, often in Norwegian, was everybody's favorite part of the annual Christmas Tree Party—as in this scene from 1927.

devised "a novel plan, whereby the student body was divided into several alphabetical groups" to distribute the several hundred presents.

Everyone's favorite, however, seemed always to be the evening's conclusion: caroling in the traditional Norwegian way, by joining hands and circling the tree. "After the program, the big lights were dimmed and the electric current was sent to the many-colored bulbs hidden between the heavy branches and ornamental trimmings of the Christmas Tree which towered majestically from the center of the floor," recounted *The Crescent* in 1919:

Science has certainly outclassed magic; when that magnificent Christmas tree appeared from out of the darkness, shining with a celestial brilliance and diffusing a radiant splendor of many-hued

* Number following first reference to a person indicates Concordia graduation year.

An article in the college newspaper The Concordian detailed the Christmas Tree Party of 1920.

ANNUAL CHRISTMAS FESTIVAL HELD LAST EVENING

Juniors In Charge of Entertainment

Every year it has been the custom of the college to give a Christmas entertainment the evening before school closes for the holidays.

Last night the annual event took place in the gymnasium at eight o'clock, with the Juniors as hosts.

Preliminary steps for the occasion were taken a few days before, when names of the students and faculty were distributed in chapel. Following the custom of former years each one bought a gift valuing not more than fifteen cents. The influx to the ten-cent stores of the two cities was, without doubt, greatly increased the days following the distribution of names.

The gymnasium was handsomely decorated for the occasion, and a beautifully adorned Christmas tree was placed in the center of the hall.

After all had assembled the program was opened by the band which played several selections. Two songs by the class chorus were sun, namely, "Silent Night" and "Out Where the West Begins." President Aasgaard gave a short address fitted to the occasion. Several selections were given by the "Ensrud Instrumental Quartette." Mr. Ensrud, our director of musical organizations, is pianist and manager of the company. This marked the initial .... of the quartette, ... congraculated by *lights and twinkling stars, a long drawn-out subdued exclamation of wonder and surprise involuntarily escaped the whole assembly. It was a beautiful sight. The canopy and festoons, stretched across the room, produced a mysterious whisper as they trembled gently in the soft vibrations of the air. Ah! What a sight, and what feeling to sit there in the twilight and look at the glory and listen to the sounds! Next everybody arose to walk in a ring around the tree and to sing the old familiar songs. It was necessary to make four large rings, one outside the other, and then, the singing began.*

The Christmas songs were sung both in the Norwegian and in the English languages, but, strange enough, it took the Norwegian versions of the songs to bring out the wholehearted participation from the students.

CHRISTMAS CONCERT PREMIERE

Since the 1890s, a variety of groups had gotten together to make music at Concordia. But it wasn't until 1927 that the college's first music club was organized by Miss Clara B. Duea (pronounced *Dewey*), a Concordia piano and organ professor. She gathered interested music majors (as well as a few community members from Moorhead and across the river in Fargo) with the dual aims of studying music outside the classroom and of promoting an appreciation of "better music" in the community. It was out of this second objective that the Music Club, which continued until war broke out in 1941, took on sponsorship of the annual Christmas music program.

Its premiere was on December 15, 1927. An abbreviated version of the traditional Christmas party, featuring skits, caroling and a gift exchange, had been held the previous evening. According to *The Concordian*, "The climax of the pre-holiday Christmas festivities at Concordia was the Christmas Concert given by the Music Club under the general supervision of Miss Clara

Duea. . . . Choral music appropriate to this season was the outstanding feature of the program." Directed by Professor Herman Monson and accompanied by Miss Duea on the piano, combined choirs sang a processional hymn, "Come Hither, Ye Faithful." Students pantomimed a Nativity tableau—which became a feature of subsequent concerts—to the harmony of a women's sextet singing offstage. President J.N. Brown read the Christmas story from Luke, and Rev. Carl B. Ylvisaker gave an inspirational talk about Christmas hymns and their origins. Closing with "Joy to the World," choirs and audience ended the first Christmas Concert of many to come at Concordia.

Concordia's first Christmas Concert, sponsored by new Music Club

Held in Old Main chapel

Conductors:	Clara Duea
	Herman Monson
Readers:	J.N. Brown
	Carl B. Ylvisaker

Talent and Style: Miss Clara B. Duea

In photographs, she's sophisticated, dressed to the nines. There was "nothing sloppy" about Miss Clara B. Duea, who began the Concordia College Music Club, which sponsored the college's first official Christmas Concerts. "She was a fine Victorian woman who loved flowers and always dressed in style," said Vilgard (Daehlin) Sorgen '31, a charter member of the Music Club. "She was never casual."

Yet the respected professor was easily approachable and took a personal interest in her students, who tried to match her up with Rev. Carl B. Ylvisaker when he first joined the faculty as a religion teacher in 1927. (It didn't work— Miss Duea eventually married someone else and moved to California in 1945.)

For years, Miss Duea led the Music Club, accompanying Christmas Concerts on organ and piano. Her students loved her; she believed in creating a happy environment. "Even when the day was gray and gloomy," said Vilgard, "we would come in to practice, and she would always have a rose on the piano."

HOLY NIGHT

*Christmas Concert moved to
Trinity Lutheran Church, Moorhead*

Conductors: Clara Duea
Herman Monson
Readers: Magnus Nodtvedt
Marie Stoeve

1 9 2 9

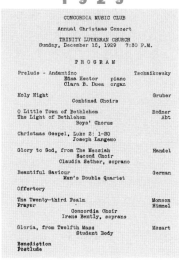

```
CONCORDIA MUSIC CLUB
Annual Christmas Concert
TRINITY LUTHERAN CHURCH
Sunday, December 15, 1929   7:30 P.M.

P R O G R A M

Prelude - Andantino                    Tschaikowsky
        Edna Hector    piano
        Clara B. Duea  organ

Holy Night                                   Gruber
              Combined Choirs

O Little Town of Bethlehem                   Redner
The Light of Bethlehem                          Abt
              Boys' Chorus

Christmas Gospel, Luke 2: 1-20
              Joseph Langemo

Glory to God, from The Messiah               Handel
              Second Choir
        Claudia Sether, soprano

Beautiful Saviour                            German
              Men's Double Quartet

Offertory

The Twenty-third Psalm                       Monson
Prayer                                       Himmel
              Concordia Choir
        Irene Bently, soprano

Gloria, from Twelfth Mass                     Mozart
              Student Body

Benediction
Postlude
```

GLORIA

*Additional music by double
quartet, boys' chorus and the
student body*

Conductors: Clara Duea
Edna Hector
Reader: Joseph Langemo

1 9 3 0

GLORIA

*Additional music by brass quartet
and orchestra*

Conductors: Clara Duea
Sigvald Thompson
Readers: Olean Rue
S.T. Sorenson

Meanwhile, the Christmas Tree Party continued to be staged. In 1932, the customary exchange of dime presents was canceled, and each student instead gave 10 cents to charity; this practice continued throughout the Depression. In the 1940s, the event became known as the All-College Christmas Party and was preceded by a formal dinner in the dining hall. Carols were still sung around a tree in the gymnasium. Eventually, this all-college function was discontinued, but the Christmas Concerts had already begun to flourish.

CHANGES OF VENUE

In its second year, 1928, the Concordia Music Club moved its Christmas Concert to Moorhead's Trinity Lutheran Church, just up the street from the college. Vilgard Sorgen remembered the scene:

We marched in down the whole aisle singing, maybe 40 of us. Mrs. Monson sat toward the front, and one of their young sons would stand up in the pew and direct—following his father's motions. During the intermission, the choir would go down to the basement, while the (women's) sextet or (men's) quartet sang.

For several years after, certain features became traditional to the concert: the Nativity tableau (directed in the early 1930s by Miss Frida Nilsen, dean of women), the reading of the Christmas story, the "Gloria" chorus from Mozart's *Twelfth Mass* sung by the entire Concordia student body and a 16-voice men's chorus singing Beethoven's "The Heavens Resound."

Other hints of Christmas Future are found in accounts of these early concerts. In 1928 an octet sang "Holy Night," while "the choir seated in the gallery hummed the echo." Echo choirs were a common feature. "I remember we always felt so crowded," said Vilgard Sorgen. "I sang in the sextet, and one year we were in a tiny little sacristy, singing to give the echo effect." Massed voices ended the evening with Handel's "Hallelujah Chorus." (Nearly half a century later, that piece would also climax the 1971 concert, "King of Kings," cited by many as their all-time favorite.)

The Concordia Sextet, comprising Gwen Ogren '30, Myrtle (Olson) Stensland '31, Maren Johnson '31, Borghild Torvik '31, Johanna Hove '31 and Vilgard Sorgen, sang in Christmas Concerts and toured the area by Concordia bus in the early 1930s.

By 1929 Miss Duea was recruiting a second choir to assist in the Christmas Concert. Chosen in late November, they practiced three days a week during the two weeks before the December 15 concert, which also included a chorus of seventh- and eighth-grade boys from Moorhead.

Into the 1930s these concerts included names that would become familiar to followers of Concordia's musical success: Herman Monson, who continued directing the first choir until 1937; orchestra director Sigvald Thompson; and always behind the scenes, until she resigned in 1945, Miss Duea. Even some of the music is familiar today: Mendelssohn's "Behold, a Star from

Jacob Shining," performed in 1988 and 1993, had been sung by the Concordia chorus as "There Shall a Star from Jacob" at the 1930 Christmas Concert. Through the years, various musical entities appeared, including not only the combined Concordia choirs, but also soloists and small ensembles, a brass quartet and the organ prelude and postlude, played by Miss Duea.

'A FAR-REACHING PROGRAM'

"Christmas at Concordia" was to enjoy a wider

CHRISTMAS CONCERT
given by
CONCORDIA COLLEGE MUSIC CLUB

Sunday, Dec. 13, 1931   8:00 P.M.

Prelude--Andantino Semplice   Tschaikovsky
        Edna M. Hector--piano
        Clara B. Duea- organ

Holy Night   Gruber

The Christmas Story
        Albert Abrahamson
Christmas Carols
Beautiful Savior   Arr. by Monson
        Concordia Chorus
            Herman W. Monson, director

Gesu Bambino   Pietro A. Yon
        John Moen, Tenor
        Margaret Olson, Accompanist
        Lucia Buslee, Violin obligato

The Heavens Resound   Beethoven
        Male Chorus
            Arnold Larson, director

Offertory- Andante from 5th Symphony
                                      Beethoven
        Edna M. Hector
        Clara B. Duea

Gloria from Twelfth Mass   Mozart
        Concordia Chorus

Postlude
        Clara B. Duea

Conductors: Clara Duea
                   Herman Monson
                   Arnold Larson
Reader: Albert Abrahamson

Conductors: Clara Duea
                   Herman Monson
                   Frida Nilsen
Reader: Willis Thompson

Conductors: Clara Duea
                   Herman Monson
                   Frida Nilsen
Reader: Wayne Williams

Conductor: Herman Monson
Narrator: Gabriel Hauge

'Prestige in Music': Professor Herman W. Monson

Credit for much of the early recognition of Concordia's music program belongs to Herman W. Monson, who became head of the college's music department in 1923 and was a member of the faculty until 1937. "Monson's efforts in connection with the Concordia choir have brought to that organization the recognition of the outstanding critics in this territory, who have ranked it among the select choral groups in the country," read the 1935 *Cobber* yearbook.

Under Monson, the choir made its first ambitious tour, traveling to the West Coast in 1927 and touring Midwest states every spring.

As a conductor, Monson was strict, demanding punctuality. Vilgard Sorgen recalled his reaction when she arrived late for practice, sweating and still wearing her basketball knickers. Monson looked at her severely: "Doesn't your coach have a watch?"

He was also a kind man, solicitous of students like Vilgard, whose missionary parents were far away in China.

Because of limited funds, the conductor spent hours copying small-format music onto examination paper, which was then mimeographed. Despite his frugality, he always insisted that the men wear their tuxedos, no matter how small the concert audience.

During the Christmas Concert intermission, some of the students would impersonate Monson. "He would laugh away at it," said Vilgard. "We thought sometimes they were going a little too far, but he never stopped them. . . .

"Oh, I tell you, we loved it in choir."

Candlelight and Caroling ... On the Air

G. Lydian Schoberg scripted a December 1937 "Cobbercast" to promote the upcoming Christmas Radio Party, by then an annual and growing event:

Schoberg: Into the studio just now has bustled genial and cheery Arthur O. Wigdahl, Concordia's manager of almost anything, whether it be musical or in the fields of disharmony. I asked him in here today, in fact, because I want to ask him, for your benefit, a few questions relative to the Concordia Radio Christmas Party, which it is his happy duty to manage.

Wigdahl: Yes, I have that happy privilege, and it's a real thrill, Mr. Schoberg, and a genuine inspiration to all of us to know that not only radios but Cobbers are tuned to us and to each other during that happy half hour.

Schoberg: You were with me at the inception of the idea three years ago, Mr. Wigdahl. Won't you tell us something about the history of this big Cobber event?

Wigdahl: The idea came during a committee meeting from one of its members, Rev. F.W. Schmidt. The first two Christmas parties had to do with the dramatization of the history of the college . . . .

Schoberg: It may be of interest to know how these Radio Christmas Parties are planned. Yesterday students met with you to receive both plans and enthusiasm. Now if you will tell the folks at large

'Prexy' Brown lights the Christmas candle at his home during a Christmas Radio Party.

something of what you inspired into students yesterday, I believe that inspired students will meet inspired parents and friends, as they go home, to plan real gatherings on the 28th.

Wigdahl: At ten thirty that Wednesday evening, you will hear WDAY's own program director, Ken Kennedy, broadcasting through the station's mobile shortwave unit, as he walks up the street toward the illuminated college buildings, directly to President Brown's home where you will hear the description of his lighting of the Concordia Christmas candle, the signal to every Cobber party to set the flame to identical candles, which then will stand as symbols during the evening, and you will thrill next as his voice leads all Cobber voices in pledging anew their faith in Concordia.

Schoberg: That certainly will be an impressive moment. . . .

G. Lydian Schoberg hosted the Christmas Radio Parties that united Concordia gatherings in more than 200 towns. Broadcasts featured Concordia news, a candlelighting ceremony and caroling.

reach and recognition after the college aired its first interstate holiday broadcast "to unite all Cobbers (Concordia students and alumni)." Carried on Fargo's WDAY Radio, the Concordia Christmas Radio Party was billed as "a festive hour for Cobbers in the Northwest" and aired on December 30, 1935, from 10:30 to 11 p.m. Sponsored by Concordia's News Bureau, the broadcast was directed by Gabriel S. Hauge '35, assistant dean of men and debate coach.

Behind the Radio Party was the idea that students on vacation in communities around Minnesota and North Dakota would hold parties "at some home of a Cobber student in the community, and a feature of this party will be the Concordia broadcast from the chapel platform over the Fargo station." What did they hear, those students, alumni and friends gathered around their radios? That first Radio Party featured greetings from President Brown as well as musical numbers by Concordia students from Fargo and Moorhead. Students attending the broadcast—and those listening—closed the program by singing the "Hymn to Concordia," composed by Monson.

Eventually, the broadcasts were expanded and carried by KFYR Radio in Bismarck, North Dakota. By 1942 individual student chairmen were selected each year to coordinate Radio Parties held in the more than 200 communities that were home to Concordia students. G. Lydian Schoberg, a professor of languages, arranged and hosted the radio broadcasts, describing highlights of campus life and interviewing various personalities. Each year, the Radio Parties included a traditional candle lighting in his home by President Brown (as Cobbers at community Radio Parties followed suit), greetings, skits, music by the Concert Choir and a meditation on the Christmas story.

For Rachel (Schoberg) Hiebert '59, the Christmas Radio Party of 1937 told a story of not one birth, but

two. Her father, none other than Professor Schoberg, "had taken my mother to St. Luke's Hospital and left her there," said Rachel, who remembered attending Christmas parties in the old gym. "He then hurried back to emcee the Christmas broadcast. I was born during the broadcast. My mother was disgusted with him because he didn't announce the birth on the air."

As did many others, Rachel's family always listened to the broadcasts while enjoying Christmas refreshments. She and her sister, Borghild (Schoberg) Jacobson '54, even sang on the air during the 1956 Radio Party. "These radio broadcasts sometimes interfered with my birthday celebrations," Rachel lamented.

Concordia's Christmas Radio Parties ceased during the war years, but were revived in 1946 and continued until 1961.

Featured Fergus Falls native and concert pianist Margaret Minge

First Christmas Radio Party

Conductor:	Herman Monson
Narrator:	Gabriel Hauge

Choirs included Trinity Lutheran's

Conductor:	Herman Monson
Narrator:	Gabriel Hauge

Gabriel S. Hauge, Concordia's assistant dean of men and debate coach, hosted the 1935 Christmas Radio Party.

Radio Broadcast Dec. 30 To Be Feature of Parties

Yule Record To Be Picture of Main

The Christmas Record will not be a publication of the usual eight or ten pages, but it will be a portrait card carrying the scene of the administration building of the college in the Cobber colors. This record comes out today.

Besides the picture, a greeting will be inscribed and an announcement will be made of the second semester. The inscription will read, "Concordia college during this festive season wishes to extend its genuine appreciation for the support and favors of the past year, and it takes pleasure in announcing the opening of the second semester 1936."

Students, Alumni To Gather For Cobber Celebration On Air Program

NEWS BUREAU IS SPONSOR

Greetings From Brown, Others To Be Heard on Radio Presentation

A new feature for the Concordia students during the Christmas holidays will be the Concordia Christmas Radio party to be held Monday evening Dec. 30 from 10:30 to 11:00 p. m. This broadcast will be made over station WDAY, Fargo.

This party is being sponsored by the Concordia News Bureau and is under the direction of Mr. Gabriel S. Hauge, assistant dean of men and debate coach at the college.

Broadcast Is Party Feature

the various communities

THE

CONCORDIA MUSIC CLUB

Sponsors Its

ANNUAL

CHRISTMAS CONCERT

First Lutheran Church

Fargo, No. Dak.

Sunday, December 12th

7:45 P. M.

1937

Held at First Lutheran Church, Fargo (alternating with Trinity in Moorhead until 1942)

Paul J. Christiansen's first year at Concordia

Conductors: Paul J. Christiansen
Clara Duea
Sigvald Thompson

Reader: Fredrik Schiotz

A NEW ERA BEGINS

In 1937 Herman Monson was succeeded by Paul J. Christiansen as chair of the music department. That same year, the Christmas Concert, under the direction of the new young conductor (and the ever-present Miss Duea), was held in First Lutheran Church in Fargo. For the next five years, as its audience continued to grow, it alternated between First Lutheran and Trinity. President Brown's fears that the churches wouldn't be filled were unfounded. They were filled to overflowing. "We believe a change necessary," proclaimed *The Concordian* after the first year:

> To the 1,200 people who crowded the First Lutheran church Sunday evening the annual Christmas concert was thrilling. But to the hundred or more who were unable to get in, the program was a complete failure. To the several hundred more who had to sit or stand in the aisles it is obvious the program could not be the completely enjoyable concert it might have been.
>
> There are several possible remedies. It is obvious something must be done to make this musical treat available to the audience which can listen with at least a minimum of physical comfort. One possibility would be to hold the annual affair in a larger auditorium, perhaps the Moorhead armory. This suggestion, however, would remove the worshipful atmosphere so essential to the success of the concert.
>
> A more generally desirable suggestion is already in use at St. Olaf where the Christmas concert is presented twice. The first presentation is given the Saturday evening before school disbands for the student body and citizens of Northfield. Then, on Sunday evening, the concert is repeated for the benefit of outsiders who came more than 2,000 strong this year.
>
> It is obvious that more people can be accommodated this way and each listener will be more comfortable. Should such a program be adopted here? *The Concordian thinks so. It is up to the Music Club.*

Paul J. Christiansen brought a strong musical tradition to Concordia in 1937. He cited his father, F. Melius Christiansen, and the great conductor Demitri Metropolis as the primary influences on his musical career.

In his early years at Concordia, Paul Christiansen conducted both choir and orchestra.

Even as the Christmas Concerts continued their growth under Christiansen, it would be some years before *The Concordian's* editorial demand was met.

Christiansen had been a newlywed in the summer of 1937, studying at New York's Eastman School of Music and just beginning to think about supporting a family: "So, at the age of 22, my wife and I bought a Buick car for $81 and put all our belongings in it and set sail for Moorhead, Minnesota."

Although young, Christiansen was neither unfamiliar with Concordia, nor with what he could do—given a group of eager young people and good music. His father, F. Melius Christiansen, had long conducted the choir at St. Olaf College in Northfield, Minnesota—and had revolutionized American choral music by cultivating a European *a cappella* style. "Paul J." (as his colleagues and friends called him) would always credit both his father and the famous conductor Demitri Metropolis as having the greatest influences on his life and career.

"It's those musical sounds that have stayed in my memory the best," Paul once said. "I still remember crawling in that crib upstairs and hearing those sounds downstairs—the piano. Then (my father) gave voice

lessons. I remember listening to that too. So it kind of got under my skin unconsciously—sounds."

Those were his "great memories of Northfield," he recalled: "those musical sounds, how they crept into my life and stayed there."

It was wonderful how those sounds eventually crept out of Paul J. Christiansen and into the minds and voices of his choirs over the decades to follow. Arriving at Concordia, he was concerned about the quality of talent that might be available for his orchestra and choir:

I went up to the tryouts the first morning that they were scheduled and the first person to sing for me was a blond girl and she had the most gorgeous alto voice I had ever heard. I was just taken aback; I couldn't believe that from this little school this was only the first tryout … and I thought, "Well, if it's like this, then it should be a marvelous place to work."

And that it proved to be, he added. In later years, Paul J. got tears in his eyes when he remembered President Brown's words of encouragement that first year: "Paul, I think now you can do for Concordia what your dad did for St. Olaf."

Laughing through tears, Paul continued the story: "He gave me a five-dollar-a-month raise, which in those days would buy quite a few hamburgers. I'll never forget that—Dr. Brown coming to me after the concert and encouraging me like that, because I was really so young when I came here."

J.N. Brown, who served as Concordia's president from 1925-1951, encouraged Paul Christiansen to expand the Christmas Concert event.

1 9 3 8

Sigvald Thompson was a member of featured string quartet from the Fargo Conservatory

Greetings offered by Concordia president J.N. Brown

Conductors: Paul J. Christiansen
Engebret Thormodsgaard
Clara Duea

1 9 3 9

PEACE ON EARTH, GOOD WILL TOWARD MEN

"Choric speakers" speaking choir conducted by Norma Ostby

Conductors: Paul J. Christiansen
Clara Duea
Sigvald Thompson

"Our goal is to illuminate the Word at Christmas — and that's thrilling."

—René Clausen

Chapter 2

AND IT CAME TO PASS

The Word

One of the most exciting things for us was when he frequently chose one member in the community – we would know who that person was, but that person would not know – and he would write the Christmas Concert for that person. One time it was Irv and Bud from the gas station, and another time it was the grocer or the barber. I think that person would become the face of the community – this person's anguish or that person's joy.

—Ingrid Christiansen '66

When Paul Christiansen and Cy Running began working together to plan the Concordia Christmas Concerts, it was clearly a partnership "made in heaven," according to Paul's daughter, Ingrid. Cyrus M. Running joined Concordia's staff as art department chair in 1940. It was the early collaborations of Paul J. and Cy that created the modern Christmas Concert. From then on, the concerts would deliberately combine glorious music and beautiful imagery – but they always started with the Word.

Theirs would flower into a lifelong relationship, and for the children of both families, there was an air of excitement when the two men worked together on the concert. Thorpe Running '63,

BUT MARY KEPT ALL THESE SAYINGS, PONDERING THEM IN HER HEART

First backdrop and program cover designed by Cyrus M. Running

Conductors: Paul J. Christiansen
Clara Duea
Andrew Ponder

A 1940 Christmas Concert review

ANNUAL YULE EVENT CALLED "ONE OF THE BEST"

Approximately 1,000 persons packed Trinity Lutheran church 20 minutes before starting time last night to hear one of the best choral music programs which has been sponsored by the Concordia college Music club in the past several years.

A large string orchestra and the 100-voice mixed chorus gave impressive depth to the concert, which was closed by the 60-voice a cappella choir singing "Beautiful Savior" as house lights were dimmed and a sole star shone down on the "meditating" Mary.

Two large simulated stained glass paintings covering the choir and organ lofts depicting earthly and heavenly scenes of joy appropriately carried out the program music and gospel.

Prof. Cyrus Running, head of the Concor... department. did...

Mr. Running

Cy's eldest son, remembered one phase of their "creative" process:

Sometime in mid-summer, Paul J. would bang through our back door much like Kramer on the Seinfeld show—and inquire, "Where's Cy? It's time for a ping-pong game." My startled mother would direct him down to Dad's studio, where he was drawing. As he charged down the basement stairs, Paul would yell, "Cy, ping-pong!"

Then, for a good two hours, we would hear them literally bouncing off the walls of our recreation room. After the game, Paul would bound back up the stairs, out the back door and return to the piano at his house. Dad would come up, beaming and covered with sweat, to tell my mother, "Well, El, we have the Bible texts for the concert. Paul has already started composing the first choir piece, and I'm going to have the first drawings ready next week."

Christiansen described Running's 1949 backdrop: "It was a wonderful scene depicting a cathedral, and the people were so dumbfounded by this picture that they would come up after the concerts and feel it to see if it was really a cathedral or not."

President Brown was so moved by one of their first Christmas collaborations that he summoned the pair to his office after the con-

certs. At that meeting, Brown advised them that he wanted them to do the Christmas Concert in *exactly* the same way every year. This posed a creative dilemma. How did they respond? "We did the best we could," Christiansen noted wryly, "but it was never the same."

In fact, it was the newness and excitement of a different emphasis each year that provided "half the fun" for their creative minds—a statement that still holds true for concert planners today. In the early years of the Christmas Concerts, including Paul J.'s first few as conductor, a local pastor often read the narration, which generally consisted of the Nativity passage from Luke 2. With the addition of a visual component, "that started to change immediately," Christiansen said, "because the use of the visual became much more impor-

Cy Running and Paul Christiansen often worked together on their shared vision for the Concordia Christmas Concerts. As backyard neighbors, they collaborated throughout the year, at Paul's piano—or at the ping-pong table in Cy's basement.

tant, and in doing that, it also stimulated the interest in the texts that were used." Gradually, Christiansen and

Five successive full houses distinguished the 1949 concert at the Moorhead Armory.

Running worked to integrate other related texts in addition to the Gospel passages—illustrating them "in the artist's eyes" and integrating them into the music.

TEAMWORK

At first, the two pulled together a few Bible passages. But within a few years, the process became more complex, starting with ideas that generated a primary theme and involving a written script that included various biblical passages and narration. That textual element, said Haakon Carlson '62, gives "a dimension of sacredness . . . that what we are watching and hearing is the true meaning of Christmas."

Ideas for the theme were developed throughout the year. As his children grew

older, Paul J. increasingly solicited their opinions about current events, just as he did with his choir on bus tours: "What's going on in the world? What's important in your lives? What do you think is important to say this year?"

"He would really get in our faces about it," said his daughter, Ingrid. "That was his gift to the community, that he was thinking about what the community was thinking."

Never working in isolation, Christiansen often absorbed thematic ideas from his conversations with various people he met during the course of a day. "He would engage everybody in conversation," Ingrid explained:

> He would be talking with the man who came to read the meter, and some part of that conversation would give him the spark. He knew then what he wanted to say.
> He would sit at a table in a restaurant and almost badger the waitress. He wanted to know about her life and what she thought about things. He'd joke with her and kind of get her going—but he would be fed by those exchanges with people. So the concert was sort of a meeting place

Concordia College Christmas Concert

This little child shall be the joy of all the earth++

FIRST LUTHERAN CHURCH, FARGO
DECEMBER 14, 1941

THIS LITTLE CHILD SHALL BE THE JOY OF ALL THE EARTH

Christmas Concerts were choir-sponsored for the first time

All a cappella music

Chapel Choir reorganized as women's chorus due to shortage of men during the war

Conductors: Paul J. Christiansen
Kathryn Dean

Paul J. penciled time notations on his copy of the script.

7 min. music this page including recessional. Hem

this is our God

Page 7

Nar.: In that day the people will proclaim: This is our God, in whom we trust, this is our God, for *Hem* whom we have waited! This is our God! Now at last he is here! What a day of rejoicing! Listen to them singing! In that day the whole world will sing this song: Our city is strong! We are surrounded by the walls of salvation! Open the gates to everyone. For all who love the Lord may enter here! Tears of joy shall stream down their faces as I lead my people home.

Choirs: Ye shall go out with joy, and be led forth with peace. The mountains and the hills shall break forth before you into singing, and all the trees of the

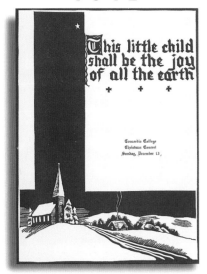

THIS LITTLE CHILD SHALL BE THE JOY OF ALL THE EARTH

First concert at new Moorhead Armory

Conductors: Paul J. Christiansen
  Cyrus M. Running

War Years

World War II left Paul J. Christiansen with "some holes in his backfield," according to Wayne Wagstrom '48, as many of the young men on campus enlisted in the armed forces. Art professor Cy Running, who was responsible for the mural backdrops for the concert, was also gifted musically. So he was tapped to direct some musical organizations including the Chapel Choir during the war.

After the reserves were called up in 1942, Paul J. had to rebuild his choir. "Without losing hope, Mr. Christiansen again painstakingly tried and retried voices," reported *The Concordian*, "and emerged with a choir based on the old standards." There may have been a few exceptions— but war is hell. His "three-note men" were allowed to sing three notes, and came in only when those notes appeared—rather like the way handbells are played. At one point, Paul J.'s male choir members were also the second string on the shorthanded Concordia basketball team coached by his brother, Jake. They were known as the "Choir Five."

Wayne Wagstrom sang in several Christmas Concerts and later became a music department manager.

Don Bentley '42, student manager of the choir, expected to go right into the service after graduating early. Christiansen was "taken aback" when Bentley came to bid him farewell. "He discovered that there might be some opportunity for postponing call-up, so he immediately got in touch with the local selective service board," Bentley recalled. "Lo and behold, I was granted a delay so I could go on the choir trip with the choir and enter the service when I got back." Bentley spent three and a half years in the Pacific; it was a decade before he saw another Christmas Concert.

For Crystal Olson Peterson '45, the war years presented both emotional and musical difficulties:

We were members of the choir, band and orchestra who had to carry on without our classmates who were in the military, or who had been killed in action. We had to walk everywhere for rehearsals and concerts. My task every concert was to be ready to play "Silent Night" on the tubular chimes in whatever key the choir happened to end their final anthem. Paul J.'s plan was that the choir would end in the key of C, but there were times when it turned out to be C-flat or C-sharp. I was a nervous wreck!

"We always trained to be selfless in favor of the whole," said Wagstrom, who felt he got into the choir in 1943 "by chance": "It was a war year, and they were desperate for men. All the 'real' men had gone to war." His marvelous year with the choir, Wagstrom said, "sustained me many times in the next three years when I was in the service." Getting back into the choir after his army stint proved to him "there was even a higher power than Paul."

During the war years, Cy Running (front center) designed the backdrop and conducted one of the choirs.

between his real focus on the gospel and the serious attention that he paid to the community—where he lived, who these people were, what their suffering was, what their joys were. He really thought about those things.

For Christiansen's family, one of the most fascinating aspects of the concert's theme was that the conductor—unbeknownst to anyone in the choirs or audience—would often choose one member of the community, and write the Christmas Concert *for* that specific person. Known only to the Christiansens, this personal focus might have been Paul J.'s mechanic at the local auto dealership, and next year the barber, a neighborhood grocer or the guys who filled his tank at the gas station. Once, it was a neighbor woman over-taken by a tragic death in the family; Christiansen was moved to hear that she had been seen walking to the concert he had written "for" her.

Gradually, a pattern for the concerts emerged due, in no small part, to the contributions of Eleanor Christiansen and Eldrid Running, who were always active participants in discussion. Each script began with a prophecy, followed by the Christmas story and ending with its "application": What does this mean to me? What does it mean in this particular time and place?

Late in the spring, Paul J. would seriously begin the search for a theme. Sometimes, it came easily; at others it required a good deal of consultation. In 1981, the conductor had a difficult time finding a new idea, and toward the end of May was "getting restless," Ingrid recalled. One day, his glance lit on a framed "Prayer of St. Francis," which had adorned their kitchen wall for many years. "It's been right here in front of me the whole time," he remarked. "Why didn't I know to turn to my wife?"

"He saw it with fresh eyes, and that became the Christmas Concert theme," said Ingrid.

During the school year, and on summer days at his cottage on Bad Medicine Lake, Paul J. would choose favorite "consultants" who helped him develop his theme and the associated texts. Sometimes they were professors of religion or philosophy. College president Joseph Knutson was a strong influence and often worked to help finalize the script. Local pastors,

THIS LITTLE CHILD SHALL BE THE JOY OF ALL THE EARTH

Conductors:	Paul J. Christiansen
	Cyrus M. Running
Gospel Reader:	Ray Harrisville

Cy and Eldrid Running came to Moorhead at the suggestion of Paul Christiansen in 1940.

Paul and Eleanor Christiansen were partners in nearly every choral endeavor at Concordia until his retirement from the music department in 1986. During his tenure, Christiansen conducted 49 Christmas Concerts.

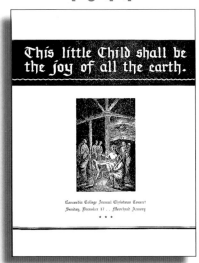

THIS LITTLE CHILD SHALL BE THE JOY OF ALL THE EARTH

Conductors:	Paul J. Christiansen
	Cyrus M. Running
Gospel Reader:	J. Melvin Moe

including Oscar Anderson and Paul Hanson, were also favorite resources, as were assistant conductors (and lakeside neighbors) such as Randolph "Casey" Jones '50, who described the process: "For Paul, the text search went all summer long. At the lake, he would be reading passages to us. He would find some good texts and then he was really a happy camper, you know, sitting there at his lake cabin."

As the script developed in the late summer and fall, the conductor would ask for additional input. Lowell Almen '63, associate campus pastor and communications director from 1969 to 1974, lent some insight into this process:

I was surprised one day when Dr. Christiansen talked with me after chapel and asked that we find a time when I could look over the script for the forthcoming Christmas Concert. Other than occasional conversation in connection with chapel or other events, he and I had not visited or worked together. Apparently, he had been favorably impressed with some of the orders of service I had prepared for chapel, and my use of language in preaching and writing. For litanies and liturgical dialogues, I would draw on passages from the Psalms or other biblical texts.

So began precious times when we would sit and talk about the Christmas Concert. The initial script invariably was too long. He clearly had done a great deal of reflecting on possible themes, texts and music. Extensive reading of Scripture

College president Joseph Knutson took an active role in helping to assemble texts for the concerts.

also shaped the script's preparation.

Occasionally, I would suggest Scripture passages other than those he was proposing. I also sometimes proposed alternative translations that might more clearly express the primary theme.

Almen would study the Greek text of the New Testament for possible wording of passages for the concert script. During meetings with his "inner circle," Christiansen would constantly seek "nuances, phrases, words, pictures that meshed with the original compositions and with the songs he was planning on using," said longtime campus pastor Carl Lee. "He would keep asking for more Scripture, or press for what a particular passage might mean. During these meetings, Cy would be busily sketching our discussions into visual form."

Because of its lyrical beauty, Christiansen almost always preferred the King James Version of the Bible for his Christmas Concert texts—even though most congregations were shifting away from that translation at the time. "I would raise caution on the language of some passages from the King James Version," said Almen, "and point, instead, to the translation of particular passages from the Revised Standard Version, the New English Bible or the Jerusalem Bible as more understandable. Sometimes my advice was taken; sometimes it was not. But the conversation was always fascinating."

Christiansen's 1975 composition, "Be a New and

Different Person," illustrated the composer's musical and poetic perspective undergoing the test of Almen's systematic theology:

> To express the Apostle Paul's teaching of being a new creation in Christ, Dr. Christiansen composed a piece especially for the Christmas Concert. I expressed some hesitation about its theme and suggested that perhaps the words should be, "**You Are** a New and Different Person," reflecting more clearly verse 18 in II Corinthians 5. Further, the alternative wording would express Luther's teaching in the Small Catechism's explanation of the Apostle's Creed: "I believe that I cannot by my own understanding or effort believe . . . ."
>
> Dr. Christiansen did not like my suggestion. He was right in terms of the poetic strength of the

piece. "Be a New and Different Person" represented more dramatic phrasing. In my memory, that piece provided one of the heartily vivid moments in that year's Christmas Concert.

Paul Hanson, who served as pastor at Trinity Lutheran in Moorhead, was familiar with many of the concert themes, having assisted in their development during the summer. At Christmas Concert time, he clandestinely obtained a concert program in advance from the printer, so he could tie his Sunday worship to the text of what Paul J. had chosen.

In the end, the Christmas Concert scripts were usually spliced together from a variety of sources that appealed to Paul J. He once explained that, in addition to the Gospel story, he would find one other "foundational" biblical text and work with both to develop his concert theme. Using the Bible as the exclusive textual source provided common ground "for all church people, not just Lutherans." Christiansen often used several different translations—his office housed shelves containing many different versions of the Bible—and "he would put his own words in it, too," admitted Eleanor. "He always had his text from the Bible, definitely. But he may not have used any particular version for his words. He would put them to music, too, and sometimes he could fit music better to something that wasn't exactly the same as what was in the text."

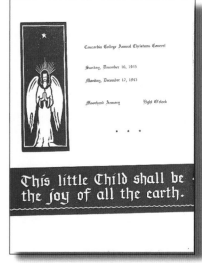

THIS LITTLE CHILD SHALL BE THE JOY OF ALL THE EARTH

Concert expanded to two nights

Conductors: Paul J. Christiansen
                   Rolf Espeseth
Gospel Reader: J. Melvin Moe

Paul Christiansen's composition "Be a New and Different Person" inspired several years of Christmas Concert audiences.

Be A New And Different Person

S. A. T. B. A Cappella

St. Paul *

Paul J. Christiansen

So be a new and dif-frent per-son filled

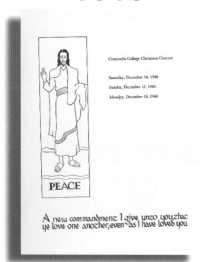

PEACE

First peacetime concert in four years attended by 6,000 people over three nights

Special lighting effects planned by Art Sanden, buildings and grounds director

Conductors: Paul J. Christiansen
Rolf Espeseth
Sigvald Thompson
Gospel Reader: Sidney Rand

Paul Christiansen's interludes were a Christmas Concert hallmark.

After one concert, a group of Catholic nuns was visiting with Eleanor:

> *They were a little puzzled and said, "What version of the Bible does he use for his texts?" I had to laugh, because I said, "The version according to Paul Christiansen."*

'LIKE A PUZZLE'

In the Christmas Concerts, word, music and art are designed to work harmoniously. Great care has been taken to assure that each aspect of the concert further illuminates the spirituality of the text.

René Clausen, who became Concordia Choir conductor after Paul J. retired in 1986, described his first step in Christmas Concert creation as "always looking": "As soon as one is over, it starts to click. When we talk about theme, I'm not only thinking musically or textually, but visually—how will it work for the mural? How will David (Hetland '69) be able to interpret what we're doing?"

Putting the whole concert together is "like sitting down with an all-day puzzle. You can't grab one piece and decide which of the other 499 pieces goes with it," Clausen pointed out. "But you begin to see how it might take shape if you get the pieces into color groups. You have to look at the big picture. I look at the concert like I do a big puzzle. It takes a lot of hours, a lot of time. And then begins the whole other process of writing or arranging or orchestrating what you've chosen to do."

Paul J.'s original interludes were created to add repeated phrases and musical

themes that reinforced the textual message and led the audience through the concert. René writes original compositions, and sometimes his own narrations, in similar fashion. Starting with stacks of musical possibilities for

Risers and mural were moved to the west side of Memorial Auditorium for René Clausen's first Christmas Concert in 1986.

the concert, he narrows the choices as he works with both music and text, asking himself, "What texts lead into which pieces that preview a coming event? Does the Luke 2 text lead up to the 'Christmas Lullaby,' or is the Annunciation text part of what this piece is talking about?"

René continues to follow the concerts' traditional pattern, beginning with a balance of slower and intimate pieces he calls "around the manger," then leaving the events of Christmas "to move toward their application to our daily lives."

That pattern, introducing and then returning to a central theme, is part of what makes the Christmas Concerts unique. Paul, said Eleanor, used a consistent theme through music and narration "from the first chime to the end." Sometimes the themes were complex; at times, they were not defined in the mural or the program, but were more subtly developed throughout the concert. Published themes didn't happen until many years into the concert series, and during Christiansen's tenure, the thematic lettering on the mural was usually different from the text on the printed program cover. In 1978, for example, the mural text was "The Power and the Glory," while the program cover read, "Ye Shall Receive Power."

Ingrid remembered one concert in which her father wanted to emphasize a sense of mystery: "It was playing with light and dark and with voices coming from offstage and behind and people descending. I don't know why he was so focused on mystery that particular year, but he felt that much of the gift of Christmas at that point for him was through the mystery." Of course, added Eleanor, "the Christmas story is a mystery in the first place."

David Hetland's first Christmas mural, "The Power and the Glory," designed in 1978

VOICE OF GOD'

Paul's son Erik said his father spent "countless hours" trying to find language for the concerts that was both understandable and beautiful. He was probably very aware of the tendency of a concert audience to tune out during speaking sections: "But he chose beautiful words, and then he chose a narrator who could all but sing those words, so that even if the audience didn't hear them, they could hear the emotion."

Early Christmas Concert narrators, always men, were varied from year to year. In the early days, the narrator was usually an area pastor, who read the Christmas Gospel. As additional concerts were added on successive evenings, a different pastor often read the text at each.

Eventually, narrators were called upon to do more than simply read the Christmas story. Paul J. would settle on a favorite narrator, who sometimes would be a part of the Christmas Concert for many years. Rev. Loyal G. Tallakson, president of the Eastern North Dakota District of the American Lutheran Church, was one of those stalwarts,

George Schultz, executive secretary to the American Lutheran Church's Board of Trustees, made his narrative style a fixture of the Christmas Concerts. Tim Johnson '71 and Mark Halaas '73 "played God" by narrating for rehearsals prior to Schultz's arrival from Minneapolis. His narrations certainly added dimension to the concerts, with a dramatic attack that gave most children in attendance the notion that God himself had spoken inside Memorial Auditorium, commonly called the "Field House." (I always thought that George Schultz was the only person I have ever known who could stretch the word "God" into fi-i-i-i-ive syllables.)

Some thought that Schultz's style was over-emotive, and Paul J. did experiment with other voices. In 1961, campus pastor Carl Lee's gentle delivery was

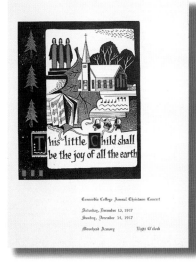

THIS LITTLE CHILD SHALL BE THE JOY OF ALL THE EARTH

J. Robert Hanson, student member of brass ensemble, later became orchestra conductor

Conductors: Paul J. Christiansen
Earnest Harris
Sigvald Thompson

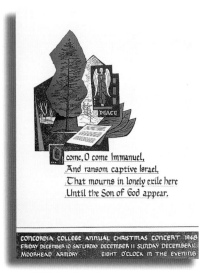

O come, O come Immanuel,
And ransom captive Israel,
That mourns in lonely exile here
Until the Son of God appear.

CONCORDIA COLLEGE ANNUAL CHRISTMAS CONCERT 1948
FRIDAY DECEMBER 10 SATURDAY DECEMBER 11 SUNDAY DECEMBER 12
MOORHEAD ARMORY   EIGHT O'CLOCK IN THE EVENING

O COME, O COME EMMANUEL

Conductors: Paul J. Christiansen
                Earnest Harris
                Sigvald Thompson

used to complement Schultz's. Lee remembered that it was not a particularly successful venture: "Paul said he wanted this reading to be like a family gathering to hear the Christmas story. Since I didn't have the voice of God, it was my one opportunity to contribute my own voice." Christiansen returned Schultz, solo, to the narrator's microphone the next year.

"While I know this relationship cannot go on indefinitely, I'm determined that it will not be terminated by my inability to meet your—and Paul's— expectations," Schultz wrote music manager Kurt Wysick in 1981.

Schultz's memorable style became the standard. Music instructor Peter Halverson '75, whose rich baritone voice has guided audiences through the program in recent years, "certainly had George in mind" when he began narrating in 1985: "As a student, I was a little in awe of the concert. And George Schultz was bigger than

Longtime Christmas Concert narrator George Schultz was presented with a Concordia freshman beanie and a Hetland mural design in 1980.

Narrator George Schultz made a rare costumed appearance as St. Francis of Assisi in the 1981 concert.

life, so dramatic—he would milk every word. I thought he was great, so when I had the opportunity to do the narration, I felt the responsibility. To a degree, I did pattern myself after George, because that was in my ear, and there was a dramatic quality he had that I liked."

For several years Ingrid Christiansen had encouraged her father to consider using a female voice. Beginning in 1979, theatre instructor Helen Cermak narrated with Schultz. Later, Nancy O'Leary, Kathy (Fischer) Valan '77 and Maura Cock narrated. Sometimes student voices, female and male, were also heard.

Like a musician, a narrator seeks the "musical shape" of the spoken words, said Halverson. When he narrated alongside Maura Cock in the late 1980s and early '90s, their real fear, Halverson said, was starting on the wrong paragraph or skipping a line. If a narrator speaks too fast, the words will tumble on top of each other, sounding jumbled to the audience. Sometimes the narration overlies a musical piece, and the speakers must pace themselves, listening carefully to the choir and instrumentalists. Paul J. Christiansen always had dialogue spoken over the music, without a musical pause, Halverson remembered: "The choir might finish a song, and then hum. If George didn't start in, Paul's arm would come out kind of flapping at his side to signal him.

"One thing that's amazing to me is that people don't know where the sound is coming from," remarked Halverson. "So there is this illusion that the voice could be from 'up there.' I think that's neat."

Peter Halverson became known as the concert's "voice of God."

'THE TEMPER OF THE TIME'

In considering not only the Christmas story, but also its application for our lives, conductors have recognized the opportunity to place the Christmas message in a contemporary context. Often, drawing from current events has helped people forge more personal connections with the Christmas story in their lives. Historical events such as the end of a long World War, the assassination of a president or the quagmire that was Vietnam deeply affected Paul J. and strongly influenced the message of some of his concerts.

When Japan surrendered in 1945, Paul and Cy discussed the need to acknowledge what would be the first peacetime Christmas Concert in four years. Finding influential events came naturally, but the theme also had to inspire both musical and artistic creativity. "Whatever the temper of the time," said Paul, he and Cy "would try to put it into an effort that would use the three artistic elements—the visual, the sounds and the text."

or unto us a child is born, unto us a son is given, and the government shall be upon his shoulder; and his name shall be called Wonderful, Counsellor, the Mighty God, the Everlasting Father, the Prince of Peace.

Concordia College Annual Christmas Concert 1949
Thursday, Friday, Saturday and Sunday, December 15, 16, 17 and 18
Moorhead Armory   Eight O'Clock in the Evening

FOR UNTO US A CHILD IS BORN

Concert expanded to four nights

Choric readers led by Agnes Risetter

Conductors:	Paul J. Christiansen
	Earnest Harris
	Robert Huhn
	Sigvald Thompson
	Leif Christianson
Gospel Readers:	V.C. Boe
	Arne Sovik
	Sidney Rand
	Sigvald Fauske

Contrasts and Contradictions

```
    I felt it so strongly last night at the Christmas Concert — the power of the hymn
"O God our help in ages past . . . our hope for years to come . . . and our eternal
home" . . . and the triumphant, victorious beat of the hymn "from earth's wide
bounds, from ocean's farthest coast, through gates of pearl streams in the count-
less host, all singing to Father, Son and Holy Ghost, Alleluia, Alleluia." I was
lifted out of myself for a moment and I was lifted above this world. And in the
haunting melody of "My Song in the Night" the person of the Christ child seemed so
very real to me . . . and so very close.
    And then suddenly it was over, the lights came on, and some people clapped . . .
as if this had been a performance rather than a worship experience . . . and ev-
erybody made for the exits to hurry home . . . to hurry back to the usual — back to
work, back to the studying, back to the struggling with unresolved personal and
world problems, back to the ordinary, everyday routines of just living. And I
wondered why everybody was hurrying so to go back to all this.
```

—from December 11, 1967, chapel homily by campus pastor Carl Lee

Sigvald Thompson, longtime instrumental conductor

Erling Jacobson

A boy was born in Bethlehem;
Rejoice for that, Jerusalem!
Alleluya, Alleluya, Alleluya.
He let himself a servant be
That all mankind he might set free:
Alleluya, Alleluya, Alleluya.
Then praise the Lord of God who came
To dwell within a human frame:
Alleluya, Alleluya, Alleluya!

Concordia College Christmas Concert Thursday, Friday, Saturday,
Sunday December 7, 8, 9, 10 Moorhead Armory Eight o'clock.

A BOY WAS BORN IN BETHLEHEM

Conductors: Paul J. Christiansen
Earnest Harris
John Moan

Narrator: Richard Evenson

Paul J. was deeply touched by the violence he saw in the world. "I felt that Paul J. was really affected by the issues of racism and the Vietnam War," wrote Carl Lee. "It was like he went back to an anchoring in some of the powerful hymns of faith . . . as he wrote deeply moving arrangements of hymns like 'O God, Our Help in Ages Past' and 'For All the Saints.' These hymns became the core and theme of some of his most powerful Christmas Concerts." In a sense, the conductor "preached to the choir," who sang that sermon with fervor. Paul J. was "a great preacher," said Eleanor. He once told a pastor friend who had been complimentary of a Christmas Concert: "Well, you know, you give one every week—but this is my sermon for the year."

During the Vietnam conflict, scripts included passages from Isaiah such as "violence shall be no more heard in the land" and "they shall beat their swords into plowshares," remembered Dale Lammi '72: "It was Paul's way of protesting what was going on in the world, a chaotic mess, and that there was hope for some kind of salvation. The music reflected that."

René Clausen has continued to take the issues of theme and text very seriously. "I think the best word is 'evocative,'" he noted. "The theme can't be too specific or too common. There has to be a sense of wonder about the title—something that evokes some umbrella of curiosity and can be developed in a number of ways. For

René Clausen continued the Christiansen tradition of composing and arranging original Christmas Concert music.

instance, I don't see how I could have 'Silent Night, Holy Night' as an overall theme because it has such locked-in imagery. It has to be able to command some noble presence—'Emmanuel, God With Us'—and be able to catch your ear and your eye in a way that says, 'Yes, now we're on to something here.'

"So I will constantly look through literature, through titles of pieces, through texts to see what might pop out as a phrase and a wonderful piece of literature, poetry—some craft of words. It's like chiseling it out of granite."

Still, according to Clausen, the passage of time has wrought some changes. "Paul J.'s programs, from what I saw, often used pages of narration—perhaps a bit more sermonizing, a bit more ponderous," he observed. "I think that was influenced by the culture of the '40s. Life was a lot harder then. They didn't have as many things. They came out of the Depression, then launched into a World War during which they had to give up a lot of other things. And so, it was a generation that was more patient in some ways, and the concerts would reflect that more patient point of view, more responsive to heavier times."

Even in more recent years, the relationship of the concert to current events has not disappeared. In 1994, with war and starvation in Somalia and an exodus of boat people from Cuba, the Christmas Concert mural, text and music fairly shouted "Magnificat, My Soul

Proclaims the Greatness of the Lord." Even in the midst of violence and tragedy, subtle questions were asked about the world's response to such terrible events. Daniel Moe '49, a former conductor at Oberlin College, originated the theme and conducted that year while Clausen was on sabbatical. Moe's experience was a homecoming he termed "a sentimental journey."

'NEVER ENDED WITH CHRISTMAS'

It is important to all involved in the Christmas Concerts that the themes emphasized through word, music and art do not disappear after the echo of the final chime fades, after the students head home for Christmas vacation, after the murals disappear into darkness. Instead, the message should have a continuing impact—

True-Life 'Magnificat'

In 1994, I saw a slide presentation by Dr. Susan Vitalis '83, who had just returned from a medical mission to war-torn Somalia. Her pictures haunted me that fall, and when interim conductor Daniel Moe discussed with me the possibility of using "Magnificat" as that year's concert theme, I knew what my central image should be.

With Susan's permission, I based the entire mural upon her photographs—and heard more positive comments than ever about the mural's message, communicated through the faces of an African Madonna and Christ child.

At the time the photograph (below left) was taken, the baby was very ill. The child's eventual outcome was unknown.

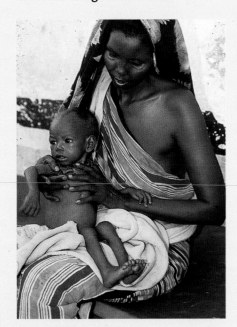

This photograph of a Somalian mother and child by Dr. Susan Vitalis inspired the 1994 concert art.

David Hetland sprawled to make final touchups on his 1994 Magnificat mural.

O COME, ALL YE FAITHFUL

Concerts expanded to five nights

Event publicized in Minneapolis Morning Tribune's "Smorgy" comic strip (see page 104)

(see page 104)

Conductors:	Paul J. Christiansen
	Donald Prindle
Narrator:	Richard Evenson
Gospel Readers:	Erling Jacobson
	Joseph L. Knutson
	Sigvald Fauske

long after the New Year rolls around and we (most of us, at least) have stopped humming "Silent Night."

Clausen feels strongly that the concert must not only illuminate a Christmas theme, but also lead away from the manger and into our daily lives, in "a kind of sending forth or sending out":

> *Our concert has never ended with Christmas— it always moves away from that event to a re- examination of the theme. So we visit Christmas in every concert, often from the eternities—from somewhere in the mystic past or Creation. We come through Advent to Christmas and away from there in a kind of travelogue. Maybe that's one way of thinking about it—we establish all of this music and text as a travelogue to guide us forward.*

Told through music and art, the Christmas Concert story is always different, yet always the same. Its relevance, Concordia president Paul Dovre once said, "comes from the fact that every year, every day is a new moment in our lives, and we hear the story and respond to it out of ever-new circumstances." Its timelessness comes from the Christmas Concerts' foundation. For indeed, "In the beginning was the Word . . . ."

"Magnificat" featured a Black mother and child along with many other contemporary African images.

The Concordian

Happy New Year!

NUMBER 7.

CONCORDIA COLLEGE, MOORHEAD, MINNESOTA, DECEMBER 20, 1927.

Sigma Rho Presents ~~en~~ House Program

~~pple~~sauce", a one-act comedy, ~~~~ the main feature of the Nu ~~~~ Rho open house progam pre-~~~~ in the college chapel on Sat-~~~~ Dec. 10. The characters tak-~~~~art in the play were: Pa, Viola ~~~~aa; Ma, Dora Gulbranson; Jen-~~~~ellie Gulbranson; and Hazel, ~~~~a Brusen. Hazel's difficulty in ~~~~ing between two suitors formed ~~~~asis of the plot.

~~~~her numbers on the program ~~~~: "Good Morning", a solo by Anna ~~~~son, selections by a quartet con-~~~~ing of Esther Longren, Kathryn ~~~~eten, Gudrun Solom, and Anna ~~~~son, and a dramatization of ~~~~"Before Christmas."

The transformation of the college ~~~~ymnasium into a busy place of sel-~~~~ng and buying occurred on Friday ~~~~vening Dec. 9 when the Women's ~~~~eague of Concordia opened their ~~~~ifte Shoppe to the public.

Birth of Christ

Luke 2: 1-20

And it came to pass in those days, that there went out a decree from Caesar Augustus that all the world should be taxed. And this taxing was first made when Cyrenius was governor of Syria. And all went to be taxed, every one into his own city. And Joseph also went up from Galilee, out of the ~~city~~ of Nazareth, into the city of David, which is called Bethlehem; ~~~~ of David; to be taxed wit~~~~ with child. And so it was ~~~~ accomplished that she shou~~~~ her firstborn son, and wra~~~~ him in a manger; because ~~~~ And there was in the sam~~~~ keeping watch over their ~~~~ Lord came upon them, and ~~~~ and they were sore afraid.

~~~~you go~~~~ ~~~~o you~~~~ ~~~~hrist~~~~ ~~~~the ~~~~ ~~~~sudde~~~~ ~~~~ prai~~~~ ~~~~th pe~~~~ ~~~~els w~~~~ ~~~~to an~~~~ ~~~~hich ~~~~ ~~~~nd th~~~~ ~~~~e layi~~~~ ~~~~wn ab~~~~ ~~~~cerning the child. And ~~~~ things which were told ~~~~ these things, and pondered them in her ~~hear~~~~ returned glorifying and praising God for all the things that they had heard and seen, as it was told unto them.

CHRISTMAS CONCERT IS GIVEN BY CONCORDIA MUSIC CLUB

CO-EDS ENJOY XMAS FROLIC

VARIOUS GROUPS GIVE CLEVER PROGRAM

Th~~~~ by t~~~~ part~~~~ Dece~~~~ wad~~~~ the ~~~~ part~~~~

V~~~~ and ~~~~ the ~~~~ sen~~~~ tra~~~~ ica~~~~ cer~~~~ old~~~~ int~~~~ Th~~~~ Solveig ~~~~ a piece; Goodie chose to become twins, who sang a duet. A silver tea at which the guests sipped imaginary tea and murmured little nothings, was planned by the second floor girls. Next came "The advantages of living on third floor" as portrayed by Leona and Inez. "The elevator is not run-~~~~ take the stairs and come up and

Christmas Chorals Sung By College Choirs

HYMNS ARE DISCUSSED BY REV. YLVISAKER

The climax of the pre-holiday ~~~~ities at Concordia wa~~~~

~~ladies~~~~ hummed verses by the chorus. ~~~~ last number of the combined cho~~~~ with Gilmore Ronning singing the b~~~~ itone solo, was Wennerberg's "~~~~ up your heads", a pompous but ~~~~ous chorus, sung with much spirit.

Towards the close of the prog~~~~ the first choir sang the familiar ~~~~ising' "Three Kings", which is b~~~~

Chapter 3

MAKE A JOYFUL NOISE

The Music

There's a hush that comes over that place when the audience hears just that chime in the beginning – and some of us don't draw a full breath until it's over, because that's the way it affects us.

—Dorothy Olsen, Concordia dean of women emerita

Even in Concordia's first Christmas Concert, held in the college's Old Main chapel in 1927, Rev. Carl B. Ylvisaker reflected on the sentiment associated with Christmas chimes. Reported *The Concordian:*

> *. . . though they are invisible to the eye, yet we love to listen to them and always await their sound on Christmas morning. Just as the church has its chimes concealed in its tower, so we have a carillon of four chimes in our hearts, namely: Peace, Good-will, Faith, and Love. Though, sad to say, they are often silent, the Christmas season generally sets them in vibration for a time at least.*

If the concerts are able to awaken these qualities, it may be because of their origins in a service of worship. Although it's called a Christmas Concert, Concordia's version of that event is,

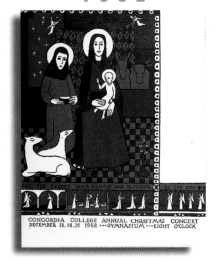

CONCORDIA COLLEGE ANNUAL CHRISTMAS CONCERT
DECEMBER 13, 14, 15 1952 ··· GYMNASIUM ··· EIGHT O'CLOCK

**AND THE DESERT SHALL
REJOICE AND BLOSSOM
AS THE ROSE**

*First concert in new Memorial
Auditorium (Field House)*

*Concerts back to three nights,
rather than five*

Conductors: Paul J. Christiansen
                    Donald Prindle
Narrator: Oscar Anderson

essentially, a worship service. During their first decade, the Christmas Concerts grew, becoming a tradition for families from miles around Fargo and Moorhead. Early conductors, singers and instrumentalists established a number of standards for which the concerts would become more widely known, especially massed choir pieces interspersed with Scripture and narration, the inclusion of smaller choirs and soloists, and the use of familiar audience hymns.

And, beginning in their second decade, the Christmas Concerts began to bear the distinctive stamp of their new conductor, Paul J. Christiansen.

He was young—and looked it. "Carl Ylvisaker picked me up one day," Christiansen recalled, "and he looked over at me, scrutinized me and said, 'Paul, how old *are* you?' And I said, 'Twenty-two.' After a short pause, Ylvisaker admonished, 'Don't tell anybody.'"

'GREW LIKE TOPSY'

His famous father, F. Melius Christiansen, had advised him, "If you can avoid music as a career, avoid it." Paul found he couldn't, later explaining: "And so, if you

can't avoid it, then you're part of it, you see."

So the younger Christiansen immersed himself in music—interestingly, training mostly in piano and orchestra, rather than in voice. Arriving at Concordia in

F. Melius Christiansen helped guide son Paul's early career.

1937, he conducted both choir and orchestra, but later admitted he was "quite more excited about the orchestra." Yet he felt inadequate to continue directing that group—which could be ably conducted by the violin teacher—and continued with the choir instead. He also taught piano and most of the theory courses, and tuned the college's pianos, besides.

Like his father, Paul found that his experience with instrumental music contributed immensely to his expectations of human voices. "He loved cellos," Paul said of F. Melius. "I can remember many times in rehearsals he would say, 'Make that more like a French horn,' or 'That's too much like an oboe.'"

At Concordia, the new conductor found a choir eager to learn and willing to stop and start as many times as necessary in order to achieve the right sound. Nearly half of the student body tried out for the choir, which would ultimately include 59 voices that first year. Paul J. was "amazed at the amount of work they would do and how devoted they were to the choir."

Paul Christiansen with other faculty members and students in 1937, his first year on staff

---

Chime . . . Chime . . . Chime

Interestingly, the chimes that begin and conclude each Christmas Concert originated with the church bells that signaled the start of early concerts.

When the concerts were moved from Trinity and First Lutheran churches to the Moorhead Armory, the chimes were retained—precisely because of the fear that the concerts might lose their "worshipful" aura in the larger, secular venue.

And so, sacred music has remained the rule.

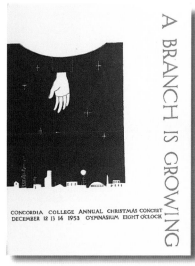

A BRANCH IS GROWING

Conductors:	Paul J. Christiansen
	Earnest Harris
Narrator:	V.C. Boe

He was also surprised at the quality of voices he found at the small college—although he would later say, "I don't think it takes a lot of great voices. I think it takes a lot of good, average singers with intelligence and musical talent."

It also takes discipline, a quality for which Paul J. quickly became noted. It was a trait he downplayed, however. "I'm not the disciplinarian," he claimed. "I think these students realize the importance of what they do and they discipline themselves—every artist has to learn that."

There were concert rules for choir members, drilled into them by conductors and choir managers during rehearsals: Eyes on the conductor. Arms at one's sides. No movement between numbers. There was even a standard procedure for fainting: if someone felt dizzy, the singer would sit down and, without reacting,

adjacent choir members would close ranks around him or her. The audience never knew anything unusual had taken place.

It was shortly after Paul J.'s arrival at Concordia that he and others decided to expand the annual Christmas program and make it into a collegewide presentation for campus and community. In fact, large crowds soon forced additional concerts on consecutive nights.

"It grew like Topsy," was how Paul J. later expressed it. "We'd do one in each church (Trinity and First Lutheran) and then we seemed to outgrow it so fast that we had to go to the Moorhead Armory to find room for people. We started with one night, and it ended up in five nights. It seemed to require a little more room every year, and evidently people liked to hear a new theme and some new tunes, because it continued to grow and grow and grow— and it's still growing."

Always Something Up Their Sleeves

Truly, there is more going on behind the scenes at a Concordia Christmas Concert than the audience ever knows. And sometimes, there's a lot more going on just behind the first row of the choir!

Over the years, members of some Concordia choirs have attempted to pass a variety of unusual items among themselves, using the giant sleeves of their choir robes for cover. Given the choir's strict rules about watching the conductor and keeping any motions invisible to the audience, one can only imagine the difficulty of passing some of these surprising objects, particularly while continuing to sing and keep a straight face.

Our secret sources reveal choir members have passed around the following items during past Christmas Concerts:

• A big tennis shoe (once left, according to Mark Halaas, "in prominent solitude, and probably desperation, on the risers following the recessional")

• A large orange highway construction cone
• A folding chair
• A woman's slip (dropped, left in a panic on the well-lit stage and picked up by choir manager Kurt Wycisk at intermission)
• A naked Barbie doll
• Spaghettios
• A jumbo box of macaroni and cheese (pasta seems popular)
• Two live goldfish in a water bottle (they made it through two choirs)

While this clandestine activity still happens, "it's not the legendary activity it used to be," said Gordon Moe, who took over as choir manager in 1989. Still, Moe admitted, "You might see a flare-up of passing items on occasion if you have a student whose parent sang in the choir."

and the word became flesh
and dwelt among us
full of grace and truth
in him was life
and the life was the light of men

**AND THE WORD
BECAME FLESH**

*TV film shown in Fargo, Bismarck,
Minot, Duluth and Minneapolis*

Conductors:	Paul J. Christiansen
	Earnest Harris
Narrator:	Loyal Tallakson

Edward Anderson '38 was a part of Paul J.'s first concert experience in 1937, quipping that "I was a senior when he was a freshman." In addition to singing in choir, Anderson played violin in a string ensemble with Professor Sigvald Thompson on cello and Carl B. Ylvisaker as organist. *The Concordian* reported: "The *a cappella* choir sang three Christmas selections and by beautiful effect of harmony and balance also added to the ecstasy of the occasion. However, the choir has not lost its great tendency to sink in pitch."

"It was a far cry from the beautiful programs through the latter years," acknowledged Anderson, "but it was no doubt the 'seed' for the Maestro's vision of the future."

One member of the choir in those early years was none other than Paul's wife, Eleanor. Asked about the experience, she laughed. She had sung under Paul's brother, Olaf, at Oberlin College, where Paul was in graduate school, and before that under F. Melius Christiansen at St. Olaf: "And then, when we came here the first few years, I sang in the Concordia Choir because, um, why not?" In fact, she sang for five years, until her first pregnancy.

Assistant conductor Earnest Harris and Paul Christiansen pose with 1949 concert participants at the Moorhead Armory.

Beneath the memorable cathedral backdrop, Paul Christiansen posed his choir before the 1943 Christmas Concert.

COMING OF AGE

R. Warren Pierson '50 recalled playing to a packed house at the Moorhead Armory.

"Christmas 1948 was cold and stormy," he wrote. Filled to capacity, the Armory lighting had been designed by Art Sanden to enhance the backdrop painted by Cy Running and the art department. There was a reading, and a speech by college administrator and music manager J.L. Rendahl during which he solicited a freewill offering, which he described as "not the noisy kind (coins) but the quiet kind (paper money)." Choirs chanted "O Come, O Come, Emmanuel" from behind a partially closed door off the balcony. "We peeked to see the throngs plodding through the drifting snow," said Pierson. "After five nights, we were tired but exhilarated by our chance to sing the praises of the Christmas season. I can never forget it, but I can relive it, as I have many a time."

Over the years, gradual college growth demanded additional music staff. The Christmas Concerts ultimately benefited from the talents of numerous assistant conductors, who directed the other choirs while Paul J. and later René Clausen conducted The Concordia Choir (also known on campus as the Concert Choir). These assistant conductors soon learned that one tricky thing about working with Paul J. was his well-known tendency to make last-minute decisions. Although he'd been working on the concert's themes for nearly a year, Paul would often change his mind, just a few weeks before the concert, about which pieces worked well together. "You didn't have much time, and you had people with only so much ability," said Casey Jones, who directed the Chapel and Oratorio choirs from 1960 to 1962. "He'd say, 'This piece doesn't fit in the Christmas Concert. You'll have to do something else.' That's the way it was."

Still, the selections for their own choirs were largely left to the assistant conductors. "He had no input as to the repertoire I chose except for the massed things," said Paul J.'s son Erik, an assistant conductor (under both Paul J. and René) from 1985 to 1987. "The things that my choirs did by themselves were completely my responsibility. A lot of that music occurred in the Luke section. And all of the Chapel Choir directors could figure out that this was a Christmas Concert, so that what they chose could be plugged into various places and fit, so it was not a creative problem." Added Lowell Larson '64, who directed the Freshman and Chapel choirs from 1981 to 1985: "One thing I really appreciated about Paul was that what he gave me to do was mine to create."

All of the conductors memorized their choral pieces, using a score only for the orchestrated works. "There's a lot to memorize, but that's part of the tradition of Lutheran choral music," said Paul Nesheim, who began conducting the

AND HE WILL DWELL WITH THEM

Artwork designed by Elizabeth Strand while Cy Running was on sabbatical leave

Freshman "Cobber Choir" started

Conductors: Paul J. Christiansen
　　　　　　Earnest Harris
Narrator: V.C. Boe

Paul Christiansen's original script and notes (left) for the 1973 concert, "Ye Shall Go Out With Joy"

Page 1　　ISRAEL IN BONDAGE

In days of old, before the birth of Christ, the children of Israel lived in darkness and despair, waiting and hoping for deliverance from oppression and affliction. Because of their own sinful and careless living, and because of their oppression and persecution of other people, these nations had risen up against Israel and destroyed the land, and made slaves of her people. Once queen of the nations, she is now a slave to other nations.

Choir: The Solitary City

The streets of Jerusalem, once thronging with people, are silent now. Like a bereft widow, broken with grief, she sits alone in her mourning. All her beauty and majesty are gone. The fairest city of Israel lies in the dust of the earth, cast from the heights of heaven at Gods command. In the day of his awesome fury he has shown no mercy even to his temple Jerusalem. He has brought the kingdom to dust, with all its rulers.

Choir: (Judah is gone into captivity)
The Ways of Zion do Mourn. The old men sit no longer by the silent city gates. The young no longer dance and sing in the streets. The joy of our hearts has ended, our dance has turned to death. Woe upon us for our sins. Our hearts are faint and weary, our eyes grow dim. Jerusalem, and the temple of the Lord are desolate, deserted by all but wild animals lurking in the ruins.

Choir: She is in bitterness.

BEHOLD, I MAKE ALL THINGS NEW

Cy Running back to design artwork

Conductors: Paul J. Christiansen
              Earnest Harris
              Leif Christianson

Professor Leif Christianson directed Concordia's band from 1949 to 1966.

Freshman, Bel Canto and Chapel choirs in 1995. Actually, memorizing the location of the various choirs, who engaged in what were sometimes called "troop movements" during the concert, provided even more nervous moments for conductors. "One of my biggest fears is always whether I will go to the right choir at the right time," Nesheim confessed. "That first year, I imagined my studio as the concert stage, and I would walk over to where the choir would be. Then June Rauschnabel (director of Tintinnabula, the handbell choir) gave me a photocopied miniversion of the program. I could fold that up and keep it in my pocket and peek at it if necessary."

'NOT JUST STAND UP AND HOLLER'

Paul J.'s choirs at Concordia borrowed some of the "St. Olaf sound" already established by F. Melius Christiansen, with origins in German *a cappella* choral music. But Paul also set his own pattern for The Concordia Choir. His musical tools included a variety of effects and compositions: sound from offstage, echo and massed choirs, specially composed interludes that were small masterpieces, the incorporation of folk tunes and an emphasis on the finest musical literature.

Separate choirs, with small groups sometimes singing from offstage, added variety—which, more important to Paul, "emphasized the text better."

"It made a more interesting musical result," he said, "not just to stand up and holler." Most concerts, observed Lowell Larson, started offstage, creating the sense of a "call" taking place. Ruth (Carlson) Summerside '48 remembered huddling with classmates behind three small evergreens, singing an "of-all-the-earth" echo to a solo of "From Heaven Above to Earth I Come."

Borghild Torvik, who taught piano at Concordia for many years, had invited two of her nieces to attend that same concert. One of them, Helen (Hallanger) Stensrud, was 11 years old at the time:

It was so crowded that I sat on my aunt's lap, my long legs reaching the floor. But the sights and sounds were wonderful, and neither she nor I complained. From the choir in the gym came "How great my joy!" and from offstage rose the echo, "Great my joy!"—then the full sound, "Joy, joy, joy!" and its echo, "Joy, joy, joy!" I turned

Conductors Paul Nesheim, Bruce Houglum and René Clausen celebrated joyfully after the 1997 Moorhead concert.

to look at Aunt Borghild, and she smiled at me, realizing how thrilled I was. Perhaps she knew I was hearing an antiphonal anthem for the first time.

Paul J. loved "echo choirs," and that, according to Casey Jones, did not mean simply two choirs singing separately. "He loved to sing down in the basement" at the Concordia Field House, even finishing up with a choir singing from the downstairs locker rooms at the end of "Beautiful Savior." In 1975, when "Come to the Living Waters" was the concert theme, choirs were positioned in various corners and balconies of the Field House to echo faculty soloist Denny Boyd. " 'The water of life, the water of life' echoed all around the Field House," remembered Dale Lammi, "and it sounded like water flowing all over the place."

Like Paul J., René Clausen has focused much of his time on arranging and composing music for the Christmas Concerts. Neither the murals nor the music

"come prepackaged anywhere," joked René (of pre-packaged art, more later). "Up on the Housetop" or "Jingle Bells" sung by the Chipmunks may be fine on the radio, but not for the Christmas Concerts. Searching for the right music to express the text often leads to the creation of original compositions.

While the conductors have always used sacred music in the Christmas Concerts, they have also been open to new ideas. Out of Paul J.'s interest in folk music (stemming from the Norwegian folksongs he learned from his father) came an interest in spirituals, which the conductor cultivated by working with an expert in Los Angeles. In the late '60s, Paul invited popular campus folk guitarists to participate in the Christmas Concert. And folk melodies from other nations have also frequently been used. From a year's leave in Mexico in 1950, Cy Running brought back a tune that fellow staff member Ed Ellenson '58 really liked. Bumping into Paul J. at coffee one morning, Ellenson asked if he took requests. "What do you mean?" Paul J. asked. Hearing of Cy's folk tune, he smiled and promised, "Yeah, we'll do that." Sure enough, that year's Christmas Concert

The dayspring from on high hath visited us.

THE DAYSPRING FROM ON HIGH HATH VISITED US

President Joe Knutson and Lloyd Svendsbye helped prepare script

Paul J. Dovre (later Concordia's president) was student concert chairman

Conductors:	Paul J. Christiansen
	Earnest Harris
	Leif Christianson
Narrator:	Loyal Tallakson

Voice instructor Denny Boyd (far left) sang a rare solo in the 1975 Christmas Concert, "Come to the Waters," for which the interlude (left) was written.

HE COMES

*14,000 in attendance
at Field House*

Conductors: Paul J. Christiansen
                Earnest Harris
                Leif Christianson
Narrator: Rolf Hofstad

1958 concert

Concordia's
Norsemen male
chorus sang
unseen from
behind the
backdrop during
the 1958
Christmas Concert.

featured a series of Mexican Christmas carols—including the tune Ellenson had requested.

At times, though, proper foreign pronunciation had to be sacrificed for the desired sound. Liv (Abrahamson) Rosin '85 was once asked for help with pronunciation of the holy language (Norwegian, actually)—an episode she recalled "with some embarrassment." Paul J. asked a native Norwegian speaker, who also happened to be in the Chapel Choir, to pronounce the first verse of "Jeg er så glad" for everyone to repeat. She did, using the more modern pronunciation of "jeg" so it rhymed with "I." Of course, Paul J. wanted the older pronunciation, which rhymed with "may." Turning to Liv, he had her pronounce the words for all the choirs.

"I normally pronounced the word so it rhymed with 'I,'" she sheepishly admitted, "—but it *was* P.J., after all."

At other times, even with the famous choir, there were difficulties with the musical sound itself. While

"Let Heaven and Nature Sing" was the concert theme in 1997.

Larry Fleming '60 was a student, he resurrected a male chorus called the Norsemen. This group had not been active for many years, but when Paul J. heard them perform, he invited Larry to have them sing a piece during the 1958 Christmas Concert. Their song was "Lo, How a Rose E'er Blooming," and this group of 40 to 50 male students, most of whom either didn't have time or chose not to sing in one of the college's organized choirs (and most of whom had trained in the barbershop singing style), was positioned behind the mural on the north end of Memorial Auditorium.

"I was standing silently among the other members of the concert choir," Larry recalled. "As they began to sing, they emitted the strangest sound I had ever heard. Paul J., who was seated facing the choir in the front row, just glared at me, and I wished I was dead.

"The next day, I bumped into Andy Anderson, who owned a nearby grocery store. He said effusively, 'Man, the Christmas Concert was great last night, especially the men's group. That must've been a Paul J. arrangement.'"

As a composer, arranger and conductor, Paul J. was constantly seeking pieces that would emphasize the main points of the text, always of primary importance in the concerts. He was also in the habit of creating numerous interludes—short pieces that linked sections of the narration and music. They were written to "fit the mood of the text," he said, "and then I tried to pick Christmas music that would fit into the text and some music that

Paul J. Christiansen directed
Concordia College Christmas Concerts
from 1937 through 1985.

YE
As in the night when
SHALL
A holy solemnity is kept
HAVE
As when one goeth with a pipe
A
to come into the mountain
SONG
of the Lord.

YE SHALL HAVE A SONG

Conductors: Paul J. Christiansen
Earnest Harris
Leif Christianson

Detail of 1959 program cover
art by Cy Running.

THIS
MAN
SHALL
BE
THE
PEACE

THIS MAN SHALL BE THE PEACE

Smörgåsbord started as pre-concert event ($2 per person for Norsk dinner)

Conductors: Paul J. Christiansen
R.F. "Casey" Jones

1960 concert

would explain the text more and express its ideas."

Those interludes were important in all of her father's Christmas Concerts, said Ingrid Christiansen, as "musical statements of themes that would be amplified and picked up and modified and bounced around the room and used over and over again. I think they would really get under your skin as a listener, too."

From the first chime to the concert's conclusion, "there was always something happening," said Lowell Larson. "There could be a theme started by a French horn, then imitated by a choir. That theme just kept coming at you. Then, in a contemplative way, Paul would take that theme and punctuate it one more time."

Paul J.'s interludes used up monumental reams of paper. He frantically churned them out all fall; when she was in his choir, Ingrid's job was to run over and copy them before rehearsals. In later years, student choir manager Mark Halaas distributed the "still hot" dittoed handouts during final rehearsals. "I think everybody who's sung in choir remembers the Xeroxed music that would appear up until about two days before the concert," said Erik Christiansen. Many of those pieces, unfortunately, have probably been lost.

To bring "a little feeling of celebration" to the Christmas-time crowds, Christiansen would always include popular Christmas carols. "Silent Night," which Paul J. called "one of the most defining Christmas tunes," was one he "never forgot from Northfield, because Dad always had a quartet sing that by the Christmas tree. That memory stayed with me." For singers in the choir, as well as in the audience, that hymn really did define Christmas. Dale Lammi recalled the scene as the choir began to sing "Silent Night" *a cappella*:

There was just one little spotlight on Paul J.'s graying head. With the flow of his conducting, he turned and invited all of those people to sing with

us. That wafting of sound was unbelievable, coming straight from all the corners of the Field House and washing your whole soul—there were guys in the back with tears in their eyes, including me. That was Christmas!

Christopher Cock, assistant conductor from 1987 to 1994, said the audience hymns were his favorite part of the entire Christmas Concert, dubbing concert goers "the most unbelievable congregation in the world."

Audience hymns and carols directed by Christiansen were a popular feature of each Christmas Concert, including this one in 1969.

Putting together the annual Christmas Concert became a year-round project for Paul J. and others involved. He enjoyed long dinners and leisurely chats with his family, playing with his children and reading them Winnie the Pooh stories. But he worked hard all year—including summers—mostly to determine Christmas Concert themes and to memorize music for the fall. Once Homecoming was over, the Christmas Concert became all-consuming. Then, after Christmas, the choir would prepare for tour (on which their conductor would often question them about Christmas themes for the following year).

After the tour, Paul J. would usually take a few weeks to travel and listen to choirs around the country, checking out performances and looking for new repertoire. And then it was summer, and back to work on Christmas. Even at his cottage on Bad Medicine Lake, Paul worked every day. "He'd take two hours off and play tennis or go sailing, but he would never take a week off," said Eleanor. On trips to the North Shore, she added, he still worked: "I remember many trips that we took in the car when I would be driving and he would be memorizing music. And he would be singing it."

His family never found his work habits to be burdensome. "Sometimes, when I was little, I would go and sit under the piano and just listen," said Ingrid, "because I liked it. I don't remember feeling as though we had to walk on eggs or be tiptoeing around. But it was expected that work was important, and you did it well."

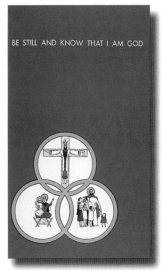

1961

BE STILL AND KNOW THAT I AM GOD

BE STILL AND KNOW THAT I AM GOD

George Schultz's first of 19 years as narrator

Conductors:	Paul J. Christiansen
	R.F. "Casey" Jones
Narrators:	Carl Lee
	George Schultz

Eleanor Christiansen's Mock Plum Pudding

After the last night of the Christmas Concerts, Paul and Eleanor Christiansen would traditionally host a gathering at their home in Moorhead for those involved behind the scenes. It always featured Eleanor's delicious mock plum pudding. She was kind enough to share the recipe.

<u>MOCK PLUM PUDDING</u>   (Carrot Pudding)

```
1 Cup grated raw Carrots
1 cup ground raw Potatoes, mix 1½ tsp.
    Soda with ground potatoes.
1½ to 2 Cups ground Dried Fruit,
  (raisins, dates, prunes, apricots etc.)
1 Cup Brown Sugar
2 Tablespoons each Molasses & Milk
½ Cup Shortening
2 Cups Flour
1 Teaspoon each of Cinnamon, Nutmeg,
  Salt and Baking Powder
½ Teaspoon ground Cloves

  Cream together shortening and sugar
  Add other ingredients and mix well,
```

```
Grease pudding molds VERY WELL!
Fill molds about 3/4 full
Pour hot water to 1 inch depth into
large roasting pan or kettle. Place
puddings on rack in pan. Cover and
steam large pudding 3 hours, small
puddings 2 hours or less. This can
be done either in oven or on stove
top at low temperature, about 225 to
250'. Makes about 20 small puddings.
Unmold warm puddings onto serving
plates. Serve warm with Hard Sauce.
```

Eleanor Christiansen

WHAT CHILD IS THIS?

Soloists represented characters of the Christmas story

Conductors:	Paul J. Christiansen
	Elliot Wold
	Leif Christianson
Narrator:	Douglas Lindgren

So, for most of the year, Paul's family heard themes for the concert and how they developed musically. When concert time rolled around, they never missed one, said Ingrid: "We were never forced to go—we wanted to go. But of course, we'd been hearing the

On the occasion of their 60th wedding anniversary in 1996, Paul and Eleanor Christiansen posed with their children (left to right) Erik, Liv (Seemann), Sigurd, Ingrid (Kretzmann) and Rolf.

music since the previous summer on the piano—we discussed it around the dinner table."

Even as a graduate student, Ingrid would arrange to drive straight from finals to at least the Minneapolis concerts "and go to every one."

"We felt sorry for the people who didn't go to all of them," said Eleanor, "because every one was different."

Erik Christiansen remembered getting into town, arriving late at a Christmas Concert in the Field House and weeping at the beauty of the sound he heard: "I had come in the south end, opposite the choir, and got the last chair, you know, so the sound was just coming right over on me (because of the acoustics created by the roof shape), and I just lost it during that piece."

As small boys, Erik and his brother Rolf chose a unique vantage point for the concerts, heading for the sanctuary of the scores of evergreens that lined the floor

and tapered up the end of the wood-planked seating:

We would go into the bleachers and sit in the trees whenever possible. Of course, the smells there and that feeling of security in those trees felt really good to us. And then the view of Dad from there was really interesting. I will always have that image of this "stickman" because I'd see him from the side, and he was (thin) from side to side, with these long graceful arms and a larger head. He was almost a caricature of a conductor from there, with the coat tails accentuating his leanness.

Everyone who sang under him, or watched him conduct, noticed how his hands and arms were so much a part of his expression. Bob Johnson '71 sang in one Christmas Concert in which the choir missed the conductor's initial downbeat:

At one point he gave us a hard cue to come in, and no one came in. The fright, the terror! He cued again . . . and again, no one came in! Then

Dress rehearsal for the 1951 Christmas Concert marked the final year in the Moorhead Armory. Concordia's new Memorial Auditorium would subsequently host the event.

'What Did He See?'

Late fall of 1963 was an emotional time. Predictably, the national shock, grief and outrage emanating from the assassination of President John F. Kennedy affected the Concordia campus as well. Sometimes the only refuge seemed to be "the sweetness of the music, the drama of the texts, the hard work of preparation, and our faith in one another," reported choir member Larry Gedde '70:

By November 22, 1963, the Christmas Concert theme had long been selected. By then, the music interludes were composed and the texts prepared. The mural was heading toward completion, and the choirs were rehearsing their music. On that date, we began to see we were a part of something remarkable, and we wondered who had looked into the future. Had someone known that the concert theme, "A Man Shall Be More Precious Than Gold," would become the perfect response to the tragic events still unfolding? It would be a concert that fit the mood of the people, and our mood, perfectly. The moment I remember so well occurred during the final performance.

If you knew him, you were aware that Paul J. Christiansen had the knack of reducing an entire concert to a few notes. The whole performance would eventually come down to just one phrase, one musical thought. And that phrase always led to a musically more intense and dramatic moment. It was the reason for everything that had been said and sung.

That night, our words rang out more intensely than ever before: "Everyman," we sang. "Everyman shall walk in the name of the Lord, forever."

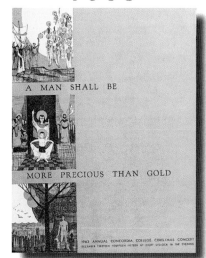

A MAN SHALL BE MORE PRECIOUS THAN GOLD

Concert presented just after the assassination of President Kennedy

Conductors: Paul J. Christiansen
                     Paul Dove
                     Leif Christianson
Narrator: Rolf Hofstad

Cy Running's original drawing for the 1963 concert mural

I recall the energy that seemed to move through the entire choir as that moment of musical climax came. Paul J. asked us to make the transition, from one chord to the next. As we did—as the word "Everyman" came from our mouths—I saw him react. I think he clutched at his heart. His eyes were fixed on the mural, above and behind us. In an instant, this incredible intensity was replaced by an astonishing serenity. From that moment until the concert ended, I believe he hardly knew we were there. He conducted almost instinctively—while we sang with power and feeling.

The gentle ending melody of "Everyman" segued into the concert finale, the beautiful "O Day Full of Grace"—powerful and dramatic in its own way. But it seemed to me that his heart had been captured by a vision which would not release him. I wanted to turn around right then and there—to see for myself what Paul J. had seen. But of course, I didn't.

I had many opportunities to ask him over the years—but I never did. A Christmas doesn't pass without the memory returning. And with it comes the question I still ask myself: "What did he see?"

Paul Christiansen's 1963 Christmas Concert composition

**TRULY THIS IS
THE SON OF GOD**

Conductors:	Paul J. Christiansen
	Gordon Carlson
	John d'Armand
	Minard Halverson
Narrator:	Loyal Tallakson

he grimaced, and cued us a third time with his "delayed" entrance cue: a closed-fist entrance cue like you've never seen, and on the back cue we all came in, just as if it had been planned that way. I'll never forget those moments of absolute focus on the man and the terror of the moment. It was like 65 points of light all focused on the hands. How can we ever forget those hands?

When he conducted, Paul J. used his whole body rhythmically, even clapping his hands, slapping his thigh or stomping a foot. "It was his style all along," said Ingrid. "He was a wonderful dancer, and his whole conducting style was dancing in a sense. If he really got into the rhythm, he clapped— and it was like dancing."

It was exciting for audiences, who saw clearly when Paul J. was swept up by the music. Choir members, on the other hand, quickly learned not to be carried away, but to concentrate wholly on their animated conductor—whose sister Elsa dubbed him "Old Rubberface" because of the many expressions he used while directing. "He could almost control the choir with a raised eyebrow," said Ingrid, "especially if you were, God forbid, out of tune or something." One glance from those piercing eyes, and "people would shape up."

When the choir did well, that was apparent, too, with pride and satisfaction reflected in the conductor's face. "Then when he would take a bow, he would often turn around and look at us and give a little twinkle or a

Student manager Bob "BJ" Johnson directed traffic while Paul Christiansen reviewed his notes during a 1968 rehearsal.

little nod or some acknowledgment," said Ingrid.

CLASSICAL BRASS

In the early years under Clara Duea and Herman Monson, the Christmas Concerts had been accompanied by a variety of instruments: organ, piano, strings, woodwinds and brass. Under Paul J., the concerts moved to a largely *a cappella* choral format, with any instrumentation usually in the form of solo instruments or small ensembles.

Paul J. had used single instruments and ensembles before, but "not a big mass of brass," said Casey Jones, whose two choirs performed C.P.E. Bach's "Holy Is God," a nine-minute number with brass, in 1961. "We had the longest piece, softest piece, loudest piece and fastest piece," Jones remembered with a chuckle. "That kind of stole the show."

From then on, Paul J. often used massed choirs with brass, enjoying the "more decisive sounds" of the instruments. When they weren't playing, instrumentalists frequently enjoyed the view. Joan Flewell Pennock '52, a horn player, was mesmerized from her spot in the balcony of the Moorhead Armory: "Concert Choir was in the back balcony ready to sing. 'Christy' gave the downbeat. Nothing happened! Again—nothing! The third time Christy, almost doing a back-bend, sparked a miraculous, gloriously unified entrance. What a phenomenal choir!"

Other brass players also noticed the physicality of Paul J.'s conducting. "We were *right* in front of Paul J. directing," said trumpeter Pam (Haugstul) Humphrey '80, "when he became so animated he dripped and shook sweat on us during the performance. It was quite a shock at first!"

Instrumentalists have had equally interesting times with René Clausen at the helm. During a Homecoming concert, orchestra conductor J. Robert Hanson had accidentally thrown his baton into the air, narrowly missing a string player. In the band room during a Christmas Concert rehearsal that year, René did the same, recalled Karl Maurer '90. Choirs and orchestra erupted with laughter at Rene's only comment: "I've been studying with Dr. Hanson."

Playing largely as accompanists was sometimes a difficult adjustment for the orchestra. "We work very hard to get the students in the orchestra accustomed to accompanying," said Bruce Houglum, who took the orchestra baton in 1995. "We have to play *so* softly, and that's one of the hardest things in the world to do."

While rehearsing, the orchestra often had considerable time during which they weren't playing. "Usually, during one of the rehearsals, we arranged to have hot chocolate or apple cider," said Lori Borgeson '92. "We would set up a large coffee pot in back of the sec-

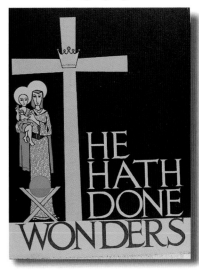

HE HATH DONE WONDERS

Conductors:	Paul J. Christiansen
	Gordon Carlson
	Phyllis Wallin
	Leif Christianson
	Minard Halverson
Narrator:	George Schultz

Full of Surprises

Many choir members gleefully recall a time the brass ensemble got Paul J. Christiansen's goat during a Christmas Concert rehearsal.

It was 1984, and with four choirs ready to line up in the aisles for the section of traditional carols, Paul J. had taken his post in one of the Field House stairwells, looking out at the auditorium. Music professor Russell Pesola, who conducted the college band and led the brass ensemble, got up to start the brass on a New Ulm-German-polka-oompah-flavored arrangement of "Good King Wenceslas." Dale Lammi, who was choir manager at the time, recalled:

They started out "pum-pum-pum-pum" and went into the Budweiser jingle, and there were about three or four seconds of blank stare on Pesola's face when he finally quit conducting and the band kept playing. I remember watching Paul J. screw up his face and look out around the stairwell. And then he finally got it, as to what the song was, and just shook his head with this funny grin on his face, and of course, we had to go back and do it again.

Paul Christiansen conferred with band director Russell Pesola during rehearsal.

1965 concert

**ARISE, SHINE, FOR
THY LIGHT IS COME**

Conductors: Paul J. Christiansen
Cornell Runestad
Minard Halverson
Narrator: Loyal Tallakson

ond violins and pass cups around until we each had one. Eventually, we would pass some up to the conductors, much to their surprise." At other times, pizza was ordered, with strict instructions for delivery to the tuba player, who was on the end of the row. "My impression is that Mr. Clausen wasn't exactly happy with us at those times," said trombonist Matthew Linkert '95. "But let me tell you, there was nothing more satisfying than chowing down those pizzas, the beauty of those murals surrounding us—and the stifled cries of jealousy from the singers behind us."

A SPECIAL BOND

Like his father, Paul J. took as his ideal the task of bringing amateur musicians to the status of professionals, a responsibility René has been equally eager to shoulder. For many of their students, coming from small high schools with limited experience of

J. Robert Hanson conducted the Concordia Orchestra from 1966 until his retirement in 1995.

In recent years, concerts have expanded from a small brass ensemble to the full college orchestra.

"serious music," the distance to that professional level is great. Helping them understand the unfamiliar music and how to use their voices to produce it in a professional manner is the task of the conductor. And that kind of effort produces a genuine bond between conductor and choir.

"When you work hard and even suffer a little with people, you become closer to them," Paul J. said. "When you strive to do something well and you try to figure out ways to do it better and you work at it—you're bound to like the people who will expend their energy in this same interest. So you do become attached to each other—the students—I to them, they to each other."

Part of the work of the conductor is to bring musical skills to students who, according to Lowell Larson, "may have been exposed to choral music, but haven't been involved in creating the heart and soul of it." That was something Larson learned as a student and later as a conductor: "Paul had that knack for *pulling* you beyond the artistry, rather than simply giving it to you. Every time that happens, you're a better person for it."

For many, singing in a Concordia Christmas Concert had been a dream since childhood. "As a young girl, I would travel many miles of frozen roads to attend Christmas Concerts with my dad," said Caren Holm-Martin '70, "and now my dream had come true, and I sang in one! I remember the year of 'For All the Saints' and the spine-tingling thrill as the basses behind me in the concert choir began that song. I felt as close to God as I can ever remember. I also remember working very hard as a choir on the pitches of that song and the determination in Paul J.'s face to make it perfect!"

Children are especially struck by how quickly the choirs move, nearly sprinting to get into their appointed places in time. Attending the concerts as a little girl, Vicki Vogel Schmidt was sometimes lulled to sleep by the softer melodies—and the imaginative child would be "startled back to life by an unmistakable flutter of angel wings brushing by me in the aisles. At least I wondered if those flapping gowns and racing steps of the choir would propel them into flight. They were *so* fast!"

Karin Svare '83 remembered sitting as a young child "in the darkened Field House, waiting for the flowing robes to speedily swish by." It was momentous for her to be one of those "swishing" down the aisles as a choir member in 1981.

Karin Denison '95 was rather in awe of the whole spectacle as a freshman in Concordia's 1991 centennial year, when the Christmas Concert was larger than ever and videotaped for national television. For her, the concert's most glorious moment emerged in René Clausen's triumphant arrangement of "O Come, All Ye Faithful":

It arrived with the overflowing crowd in the house, after all four choirs had processed to the risers. The orchestra began its traditional modulation up for the last verse, its crescendo and rallentando highlighted by bass drum and trumpet fanfares and the forceful sweep of Clausen's mile-long waving arms. Three thousand audience members rose to their feet. The chorus let forth an enormous, unison "Yea, Lord, we greet thee, born this happy morning!" while every soprano took the phrase to a high-F descant that seemed to soar on forever. It was the only moment in four years that I would simply cry at the beauty of it all.*

Singers who had the privilege of soloing in the Christmas Concerts found the experience unforgettable—for various reasons. Fay Kittelson '70 was amazed to be chosen by Paul J. to solo on a new arrangement of "My Song in the Night":

I was understandably nervous and excited as the Christmas Concert grew close, no doubt feeling the anxiety and responsibility of being a soloist for such an important event. I was also concerned that a winter cold seemed to be lurking as the weekend approached. Just in case the dreaded cough might appear, I made sure I was clutching a cough drop in my hand as we prepared to begin the first concert.

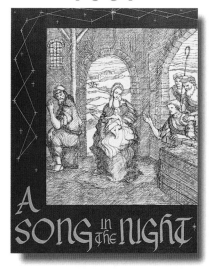

A SONG IN THE NIGHT

Mural designed by Dean Bowman in Cy Running's absence

Conductors:	Paul J. Christiansen
	Yoshiteru Murakami
	David Townsend
Narrator:	George Schultz

Choir camaraderie: Theme nights have become a light-hearted tradition for choirs during the week of intensive Christmas Concert rehearsals. Started by the 1993 Chapel Choir, according to Karin Denison, costume themes have included Christmas (with singers dressed in Santa hats and one as a Christmas tree with a star on her head), Blue-Denim Shirt Night and Hat Day. Sometimes the conductors even join their choirs in donning odd articles of clothing. Pictured on Hat Night 1994 are 1997 grads (back) Eric Jacobson, Michael Sellheim, (front) Kristi Rendahl and Jen Printz.

Dean Bowman's 1967 mural design featured panels separated by backlit, simulated stained glass.

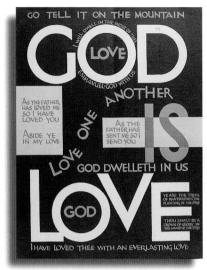

GOD IS LOVE

As in the preceding year, concert included student folk guitarists

Conductors: Paul J. Christiansen
                    Yoshiteru Murakami
                    J. Robert Hanson
Narrator: Loyal Tallakson

As was the tradition then, after the procession, the Concert Choir headed up into the little crow's nest at the corner of the Field House, where we sang the opening interludes. Sixty or more of us were squeezed into a few small rows, with Paul J. seated on a chair by the front railing. I was sitting in the middle of the front row when, during a narration and much to my consternation, I dropped my cough drop.

It landed on its side and rolled slowly but resolutely to the feet of Paul J. He picked it up and with a wry smile handed it back to me. I did make it through the solo that night, but I will never forget that brief exchange that marked my very first Christmas Concert with the man I had so admired and who made such a lasting impact on my life and career.

Peter Trier '80, who soloed in the 1979 concert, remembered:

I was not always recognized once I took off the velvet robe. After one concert in Moorhead, I was in the Normandy food service and manager Hilda Brynjulson asked how the concert had gone. The couple next to me in line blurted out, "It was absolutely wonderful. You should have heard the

Concordia College's 1991 centennial was commemorated with a Christmas Concert broadcast to a national television audience.

bass soloist who sang 'King of Love.'" I just melted. I felt my face get hot from embarrassment, and Hilda just smiled at me and said, "You want a cheese dog?"

Singers and instrumentalists prepared for the concert in the midst of heavy-duty academics just prior to the end of the fall semester. "Even though we were busy studying, we never minded putting in the hours," said Jane (Svingen) Mooberry '73, who was drawn each year to the "sights of the mural, the smell of the beautiful evergreens being hauled into the auditorium and the sounds we experienced as we rehearsed with the brass."

Working on a project of this scope also provided many lighter moments. Mark Halaas remembered Paul J.'s humorous encounters with choir member Joel Johnson '70:

On the opening night of the concert, Paul Christiansen was nervously pacing in the wrestling room in the lower level of the Field House. As he glanced again at his wristwatch, he asked Joel what time it was. Johnson responded, "If you don't hurry upstairs and get a seat, you'll probably have to stand up in front of everyone."
On the following night, Christiansen again asked for the time. This time, Johnson suggested, "Well, we've got time for a cup of coffee."

Putting the entire concert together took a great deal of planning. Rehearsals were largely spent nailing down the perfect timing among the various conductors and choirs. There is one documented incident (in 1971, to be exact) when the concert did not start on time—and the delay's source is here finally revealed by Debbie (Mellberg) Lundquist '72:

At long last, my mother and grandmother had decided to make a special trip from my home in Rockford, Illinois, to share in what would be my last Christmas Concert. It was a freezing cold and snowy day when they arrived, and I told them that since there were (at that time) no reserved seats, they would need to be at the Field House extremely early that evening. So they made their way over there, and ended up being the first ones at the door. When the doors opened, Mom and Grandma went in and sat in the very front row on the center aisle. They watched and waited while others came in, gradually filling the Field House until every seat was taken.

By that time, they had been sitting in their seats quite a long time, and they could see the instrumentalists coming to the stage and the choirs forming in the wings. Mom mentioned to Grandma that they should probably stand up for a quick stretch, since it would be a long time before they could stand again.

What they didn't realize was that both Ken Hodgson and Paul J. were standing in the wings with their hands in the air, ready to conduct the first phrases of the concert, and the person who was to strike the chimes to sound the beginning of the concert was about to ring them at that very

Paul Christiansen checked time with music manager Kurt Wycisk. The two worked together to build on Concordia's strong music program—regionally, nationally and internationally.

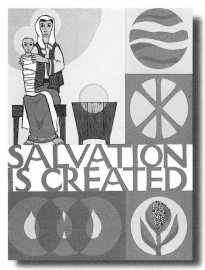

SALVATION IS CREATED

Conductors: Paul J. Christiansen
Yoshiteru Murakami
Narrator: George Schultz

Break Point

At a Field House dress rehearsal one evening in 1983, I noticed that Paul J. was sporting a cast on his right wrist. During a break, I went over to him and asked what had happened.

He explained that he had broken it that morning while playing tennis. I expressed my regret, to which he responded, "Why should you be sorry? I *won* the point!"

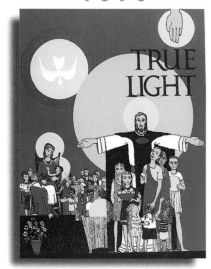

TRUE LIGHT

Conductors: Paul J. Christiansen
Yoshiteru Murakami
J. Robert Hanson
Narrator: Loyal Tallakson

moment. But . . . Mom stood up . . . and Grandma stood up. Then the people around them stood up! And row by row . . . section by section . . . the blind leading the blind . . . everyone in the entire Field House stood up in waves, like a soft breeze blowing gently over a sunflower field in summer!

For us in the choirs, it was a low rumble we had never heard before a concert, and none of us knew what was going on. Everyone was wondering why everyone else was standing up. It wasn't marked in the program. There hadn't been an announcement. The choir directors didn't know what to do either, as they didn't want an announcement to break the mood that was to prevail before the concert started.

Everyone stood . . . and everyone waited . . . for two to three minutes, until it was apparent that no one knew what was happening—except for Mom and Grandma, who couldn't stop laughing to themselves. Finally, they sat down to laugh and laugh, trying to squelch their hilarity. Then the people around them sat down . . . row by row . . . section by section . . . the blind leading the blind . . . until everyone was seated again, and the concert began, this time as planned.

It was probably the only time a Christmas Concert didn't start on time.

As they say, "all we like sheep . . . ."

When 1985 rolled around, some of us suspected it was going to be Paul J.'s last Christmas Concert—although he wasn't telling anyone. But he was near retirement, and the next year would have been his fiftieth concert—a milestone I was sure he'd never let us celebrate officially!

So we pushed (successfully) to televise that year, and sure enough, Paul announced his retirement in the spring. He enjoyed good years, spending time with his children and grandchildren, savoring days at his lake cottage in Minnesota and the Christiansen family's summer place in Door County, Wisconsin. He was an avid tennis player, hitting the courts virtually every day. Eventually diagnosed with amyotrophic lateral sclerosis (Lou Gehrig's disease), he nevertheless continued to remain as active as he could, and never stopped composing and arranging music. He died peacefully at home on December 5, 1997, at the age of 83.

'BRING YOUR OWN SHOES'

If René Clausen was worried about having big shoes to fill, he didn't show it.

A graduate of St. Olaf College who, like Paul J., became a college music professor at a young age, René was teaching at West Texas State University when he heard of Paul's retirement and the opening at Concordia. "I didn't figure I really had a shot at this job," he said. "I was still really young, 32 at that point, and I was unfinished with my doctorate at the time."

But after his years at St. Olaf, conducting at a small liberal arts college had been one of René's goals: "When the opening came up, of course I was going to go after that as best I could."

He received immediate encouragement from Paul Dovre, Concordia's president. "There was a new animal to create," René recalled. "I remember in my

Most audience members eventually stood prior to the 1971 concert . . . as this photograph proves!

Paul J.'s One-Liners

During his long tenure as conductor, Paul J. Christiansen was sometimes approached with trepidation by students, who knew him as a strict disciplinarian and a tough taskmaster. But they quickly found he had a keen sense of humor and a sometimes biting wit.

- *Paul's daughter, Ingrid, was the last person "by far" to get into the choir. "We went through nine tryouts, the altos, to get down to the last one. And then he said on that last tryout, 'I bend over backwards not to let members of my family into choir, but she did sing that better than all the rest of you . . . and we do need another alto.' "*

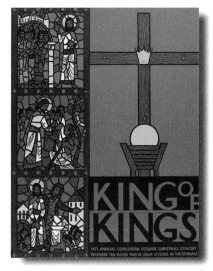

KING OF KINGS

First major audio recording of a Christmas Concert

Conductors:	Paul J. Christiansen
	Kenneth Hodgson
	J. Robert Hanson
Narrator:	George Schultz

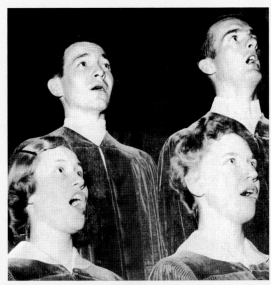

Larry Fleming (top left), Lyle Hanson '56, future Concordia first lady Mardeth (Bervig) Dovre (bottom left) and Janice (Simmons) Odegaard '56 sang "I Sat Down Under His Shadow" in the 1954 Christmas Concert.

- *Longtime Concordia College president Paul J. Dovre recalled Paul J.'s "certain way of getting his point across—sometimes oblique and sometimes fairly direct." Once, when the first sopranos were practicing their humming and it wasn't going very well, Paul J. stopped in front of one and remarked, "Bervig, you're standing in the need of prayer." (The young woman, Mardeth Bervig '57, later married Dovre—their first date was after the 1956 Christmas Concerts, at which she sang a solo.)*

- *Paul Dovre also recalled that "the bane of life for every faculty member is endless meetings"—a problem Paul J. solved early in his career by "simply not attending any."*

- *In fact, he became rather notorious for his absences. Asked to speak at an event to honor a colleague who was retiring, Paul J. addressed the crowd, which consisted largely of fellow faculty members: "This is supposed to be a recognition dinner, but I don't recognize most of you."*

- *At one of Christiansen's summer choral schools, there was a young man from Iowa who continually asked questions, dominating the class. Finally, on day five, the conductor asked again, "Are there any more questions?" There were none, even from the Iowan—at which point Paul J. turned to the young man and said, "Why, I have answers to questions you haven't even thought of."*

Paul Christiansen spent most summers leading choral schools at various locations throughout the country.

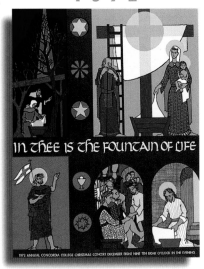

**IN THEE IS THE
FOUNTAIN OF LIFE**

*Charles Beck assisted Cy Running
in completing mural*

Conductors: Paul J. Christiansen
Kenneth Hodgson
J. Robert Hanson
Narrator: George Schultz

1972 concert

interview we discussed the fact that this wasn't a matter of filling shoes—it was bringing your own shoes."

This was an important lesson in following someone of Paul J.'s stature and tenure. "If you simply try to imitate, you can't be successful, because that person gained that strength by his own gifts and what he brought," René said. "To replace anyone who has been strong, you have to bring your own strength and your own shoes and have patience and courage and realize that things come a little at a time."

Keeping in mind that the Christmas Concerts' goal was "to illuminate the Word at Christmas," René found the prospect not intimidating, but "thrilling." Through his unique talents, he began to place his own imprint on the event.

"In retrospect, I can't imagine how it could have gone any better than it did," said Dovre. "I anticipated that it would be different." But for some people, even a slightly different musical approach varied a tradition they didn't want changed. "As René came to know this tradition, he put his own self into it," recounted Dovre, "and now it has a kind of definition that is powerful in

Changed Forever

Concordia College president Paul J. Dovre eulogized Paul J. Christiansen with these words at the conductor's memorial service in December 1998:

We recall Paul's gift to the church— singable anthems, hymns of the church made glorious by his hand, hundreds of church musicians honed by his teaching craft, and thousands of singers adding quality and spirit to choirs all across the land. We recall Paul's gifts to his profession—a unique musical voice, a high standard of performance and, through his compositions, a lasting contribution to the literature of sacred music. And Paul's gifts to the college were numerous. We note especially his standard of musical excellence which extended the name of the college and projected a standard of quality which encouraged all of us, whether we taught physics or math, French or English, sociology or speech. And then there were Paul's gifts

to his students. He inspired, encouraged and cajoled you—and why? So that you would give life to your talent and thereby you would find a vision of excellence, a discipline of stewardship, perhaps incomparable to anything you experienced before or since.

Call it charisma or genius or persistence

or whatever you will, but he drew it out of you—your talent, your loyalty, your passion—and you have never since been what you once were.

its own right." Added choir manager Gordon Moe '89: "I don't think he's ever looked back. I think he respects what Paul J. did, but he's doing his own thing."

Christmas Concerts provided Clausen with the opportunity to explore and expand his creative horizons. Occasionally, he would experience a moment that was "tremendously special," as during the 1995 concert, when his young daughter Katie sang "Keep Me as the Apple of Your Eye":

René Clausen came to Moorhead in 1986 to lead The Concordia Choir and direct the Christmas Concerts.

That concert had contrast built into it with this child's pure voice. To be able to conduct her there with the string orchestra and my own choir in the background answering her voice was a very special experience.

She had no nerves. She was at a time of her life when it didn't matter if there were 4,000 people there—she just s-a-a-n-n-g this piece. I remember coaching the college singers how to handle nerves and the television. And sometimes you have to be a child to realize that you just allow your voice to sing. She didn't feel scared—she thought, "I'll just sing to Dad out there."

She was 10 at that point and still sat on Dad's knee. . . . I look nostalgically back at that time, knowing that it won't come again.

ADDING COLOR

One major change under René was the addition of the full orchestra. Brass choirs at Christmas, Paul J.'s

tradition, "are like Christmas caroling, they're like apple pie and Mom—they all go together," René acknowledged. But from a musical standpoint, the new conductor felt the orchestra opened up many more possibilities: "The music that we might do with combined choir is appropriate for full orchestrations. We will do movements from oratorios, movements from large works. For instance, to do 'For Unto Us a Child Is Born' from *Messiah* is much nicer with orchestra as Handel wrote it—with the strings and the winds."

Interestingly, Clausen spoke of instruments and voices using the metaphor of color—just as Paul J. and F. Melius Christiansen had done: "You keep adding to the palette. The orchestra has really added a lot in terms of shaping the colors—instead of using just primary colors, we've got some pastels that we can throw in." Strings, for example, might be used to create a "halo of sound" appropriate for a lullaby, or woodwinds to sound an obligato counter melody or transition.

"And now it's changed again with the addition of the Tintinnabula, the bell choir, as another color," René said. "As they've been in the concert longer, I've learned to refine, how to use them more effectively and how bells, or one bell, may have another kind of effect."

Both conductors, Christiansen and Clausen, have brought their own musical ideals to the modern Christmas Concert. Peter Halverson, who sang in Paul J.'s choirs as a student, recalled the way in which Christiansen "would transport you" as a singer, part of it stemming from the influence of Metropolis and the other great,

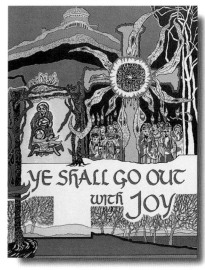

YE SHALL GO OUT IN JOY

Paul Allen designed artwork for the first time, after Cy Running's health forced his retirement

Conductor: Paul J. Christiansen
Narrator: George Schultz

Young Katie Clausen sang "Keep Me as the Apple of Your Eye" in the 1995 concert.

BEHOLD, I AM COMING SOON

*First performances at Orchestra
Hall in Minneapolis*

Conductors: Paul J. Christiansen
             David Townsend
             Robert Baily
Narrator: George Schultz

romantic-style conductors: "Some people thought it was all about P.J., but it was not—it was always about the music, and beyond. He went somewhere else in his mind, and that's where he conducted from. You could feel it so intensely, you were just drawn to it—he would

The Mysterious Claude-Michel D'Etoile

1995's Christmas Concert, "In the Shadow of Your Wings," featured an orchestral prelude by a little-known composer, Claude-Michel D'Etoile. Translated as Claude-Michel "from the stars," the name was actually a pseudonym coined, somewhat tongue-in-cheek, by conductor/composer René Clausen as a reference to one of his favorite shows, *Star Trek*. "I thought, if David Hetland can do the quail under a bush *(see page 85)* and all the other (whimsical objects) that I remember fondly, I could have my own little fun."

It didn't end there. In the prelude, the Trekkie conductor used as a musical bridge the main opening of the original *Star Trek* series, cleverly concealed in the orchestral number. During rehearsals at Orchestra Hall, the trumpet came in on the "Trekkie" section as narrator Peter Halverson's "voice of God" boomed: "To boldly go where no man has gone before!"

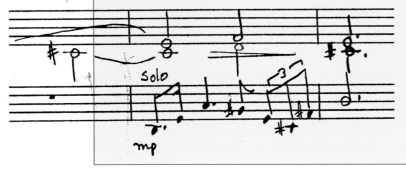

take you where he was."

Clausen, a wonderful combination of the analytical and the creative mind, senses "both the structure of a piece and the heart of it," said Halverson.

"But the amazing thing is, I don't think we could have found a conductor more like P.J. than René. They both really do it their way, and they don't apologize for it. They don't follow a certain trend or style. I think René looks back on P.J. in terms of what you have to have to maintain that program—an absolute commitment. And that's something that René has: an absolute commitment to his music."

Tintannabula, the handbell choir, made its Christmas Concert debut under the direction of June Rauschnabel in 1996.

DAYS FULL OF GRACE

Following Paul J. Christiansen's death on the opening day of the 1997 Christmas Concert, Rev. Ernie Mancini and President Dovre announced his passing at the traditional President's Dinner that evening. "It was a poignant time," Dovre recalled. "Coming when it did, it had such an impact on people. There was such a graciousness about it, and those of us who had been close to Paul . . . thought of it as an act of grace."

Even on the day before he died, Paul J. had been working on a new composition. In the hymnal he was working from, his daughter, Ingrid, discovered notes on two pieces about heaven. Next to them her father had written, "Yes! December 1997," a notation indicating that he intended to pen arrangements of them. At his memorial service the following week, the texts chosen were from past Christmas Concerts, so that, as Ingrid said, "you could hear the music echoing through them."

It was easy to imagine Paul J. and Cy Running collaborating on celestial Christmas Concerts; many friends wrote Eleanor that they were sure the heavenly

COME TO THE WATERS

Conductors:	Paul J. Christiansen
	Kenneth Hodgson
	Russell Pesola
Narrator:	George Schultz

Final Bow for a Beloved Conductor

Orchestra conductor J. Robert Hanson composed, arranged and conducted an array of beautiful orchestral preludes and accompaniments between 1986 and 1993. Members of the choir as well as orchestra musicians greatly admired Hanson—and during the 1993 concert, when he was set to retire the following year, "every song he conducted and every comment he made was sealed away as an 'I was there one of the last times Dr. Hanson ...' memory," according to Karin Denison:

One such time was during a morning rehearsal in Minneapolis' Orchestra Hall for the Thursday night concerts. It was Felix Mendelssohn's "Behold a Star from Jacob Shining," the first piece after the opening processional, set with full choir and orchestra and directed by Dr. Hanson. It was a moving piece, and we sang it well.

When the song ended, Dr. Hanson put his baton down on the stand. There was silence. He didn't step down, but instead looked up and spoke, thanking the students for giving him "the privilege to conduct you in this glorious piece of music." Unable to continue speaking, he stepped off the podium.

As he descended the stairs to the audience seats, the applause started among singers and players and grew steadily,

along with cheering and wolf whistles. The boisterous standing ovation from 400 student musicians lasted for several minutes, until Dr. Hanson ascended the stairs to acknowledge the cheers.

When he reached the stage, however, the sixty-something conductor didn't just stand there. With characteristic spriteliness, he jogged across the floorboards and literally took a flying leap onto the podium, landing with both arms outstretched above his head, a wide grin on his face as he rotated to face one end of the group, then the other. The crowd roared its approval in an ovation that seemed as if it would never end, as Dr. Hanson—like a well-loved champion— took one of his last, well-deserved bows.

J. Robert Hanson conducted Christmas Concert rehearsals with the Concordia College Orchestra.

Detail from Paul Allen's 1975 mural

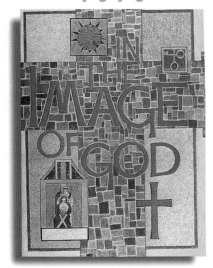

IN THE IMAGE OF GOD

Conductors: Paul J. Christiansen
                 Larry Fleming
                 Russell Pesola
Narrator: George Schultz

Paul Christiansen spent countless hours at the piano in his home studio.

choirs were singing better. "Even in heaven I think, it's hard for me to imagine that the angels will sing to Paul J.'s standards of excellence," eulogized Rev. Ann Svennungsen '77.

For students, the conductor's demands for perfection had often been frustrating—but there were moments in the Christmas Concerts that made all the challenges worthwhile. "When you get the chord right and everything seems to float, you feel like you're somewhere out of this world," said Liv Rosin. "Especially during the Christmas Concert, when (Paul J.) would be directing and maybe he'd take a dramatic pause, you would be feeling like you were just ready to start jumping up and down and screaming or yelling or crying—all these emotions all at once."

It's that kind of emotion that conductors harness to create an experience that is a great artistic performance and an act of worship, according to Clausen:

What we'll do in a Concordia Christmas Concert will always be the best of sacred music. We owe it not only to our audiences, but also to our students. When we do this concert, we're illuminating the unchangeable word of God from one generation to another—we can't do that in a cheap way.

To maintain that standard, conductors, choirs and instrumentalists must put themselves in the frame of mind for worship. Ten minutes before each concert starts, the ensembles have their own devotions for that very purpose.

"I think that we get through to them," René said. "With each pass-

Christmas Concert Top 10 Choral Pieces*

1. Silent Night (62)
2. Joy to the World (31)
3. All My Heart This Night Rejoices *and* From Heaven Above (23)
4. Angels from the Realms of Glory, Angels We Have Heard on High *and* O Come, All Ye Faithful (18)
5. Away in a Manger (17)
6. Hark! The Herald Angels Sing (16)
7. A Christmas Carol, A Great and Mighty Wonder *and* O How Beautiful the Sky (13)
8. Thy Little Ones, Dear Lord, Are We (12)
9. Hodie Christus Natus Est; Lo, How A Rose E'er Blooming *and* The Happy Christmas Comes Once More (11)
10. Beautiful Savior (10)

Honorable Mention: Advent Motet *and* Wake, Awake for Night Is Flying (8)

Composers and Arrangers*

1. F. Melius Christiansen (104)
2. René Clausen (65)
3. G.F. Handel (45)
4. Paul J. Christiansen (36)
5. Benjamin Britten (30)
6. J.S. Bach (27)
7. Felix Mendelssohn (23)
8. John Rutter (20)
9. Ralph Vaughan Williams (18)
10. Alexander Gretchaninoff (15)

Honorable Mention: Michael Praetorius *and* Melchoir Vulpius (14)

* For complete listings, see page 122.

ing year, it becomes more sacred to them until the time of their senior year when they sing the 'Compline' for the last time—that's very difficult for them."

In recent years, "Compline" has become a trademark of the concert's closing moments. Based on an eighth-century chant for the last of the seven canonical

1997's television production, "Let Heaven and Nature Sing," was the largest in Concordia Christmas Concert history.

hours, "Compline" offers a quiet prayer for the close of the day. "I think if I didn't do 'Compline' I would be thrown out by my choir," said René. This tradition, René confessed, evolved like many Christmas Concert traditions do: "We did it two years in a row." Since then, by singing "Compline" in the concert's final moments, the choir pronounces a unique blessing on the audience. "Every year when that happens, it's usually after the big finale piece, and I put down the baton," said the conductor. "It's just the darkness and my hands and their voices."

While Paul J. liked to close the concert with a huge, massed choir number—I still hear people recall Handel's "Hallelujah Chorus" which resounded at the

end of 1971's "King of Kings" concert—René takes a more reflective approach.

"It's different in style," commented Bruce Houglum. "René's approach is more like, 'Let's have them think about it, meditate—close quietly.'"

For choir members, singing the final song and hearing the chimes sound on their last Christmas Concert is a powerful experience. "I'll never forget the hush that fell over the entire Field House when the chimes sounded, nor the emotion that washed over me the last time we'd sing the final ensemble number," said Liv Rosin. "I'd grab the hands of the young women on either side of me and we'd struggle through the song, tears streaming down our faces."

Conductors, too, feel both musicality and spirituality. On the Friday afternoon before each year's opening concert, Clausen journeys to the empty Memorial Auditorium to sit alone in quiet contemplation for a few moments. There, he meditates on the meaning and power of the worship experience that will soon be brought to large audiences, and he carefully studies the mural for the visual messages it holds.

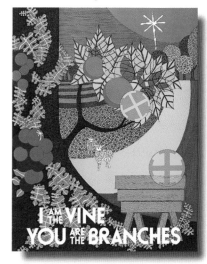

I AM THE VINE, YOU ARE THE BRANCHES

James Cermak began work as technical director

Conductors: Paul J. Christiansen
                Larry Fleming
                Russell Pesola
Narrator: George Schultz

Grand Finale

On one occasion, interaction of audience and choir was unfortunate, noted Jerilyn Forde:

Shortly before the close of the concert, a woman left the auditorium, came hustling down the steps and quickly entered the restroom. During her absence, the women's Bel Canto Choir had exited the auditorium and lined up the full length of the north-south corridor facing the stairwells (and consequently the same restroom), in preparation for the concert's final echoes. Just as the woman emerged, the Bel Canto women sang an angelic "Amen." Shocked and embarrassed, the startled lady got this dreadful expression on her face and quickly pulled herself back into the restroom—never to be seen again.

THE POWER AND THE GLORY

First mural designed by David J. Hetland, painting supervised by Dean Bowman

Concert sung by a single massed choir instead of the usual separate choirs

Conductors: Paul J. Christiansen
                    Larry Fleming
                    Russell Pesola
Narrator: George Schultz

With darkened hall and lighted mural (left), the 1998 concert's spiritual impact was clear and enduring. Full Christmas Concert rehearsals in the music hall (above) were often extremely cramped. Recently expanded facilities have greatly relieved that problem.

When that evening's concert is over, the conductors will not take a bow, nor will the choirs return to the front of the hall to bask in the applause. There are no encores. It is a deliberately quiet and contemplative conclusion, according to Clausen. "When we end and the lights go down and the 'Compline' is pronounced upon the congregation, we want to leave them with a strong, lasting image of what we believe to be true."

Bruce Houglum succeeded
J. Robert Hanson as Concordia
Orchestra conductor.

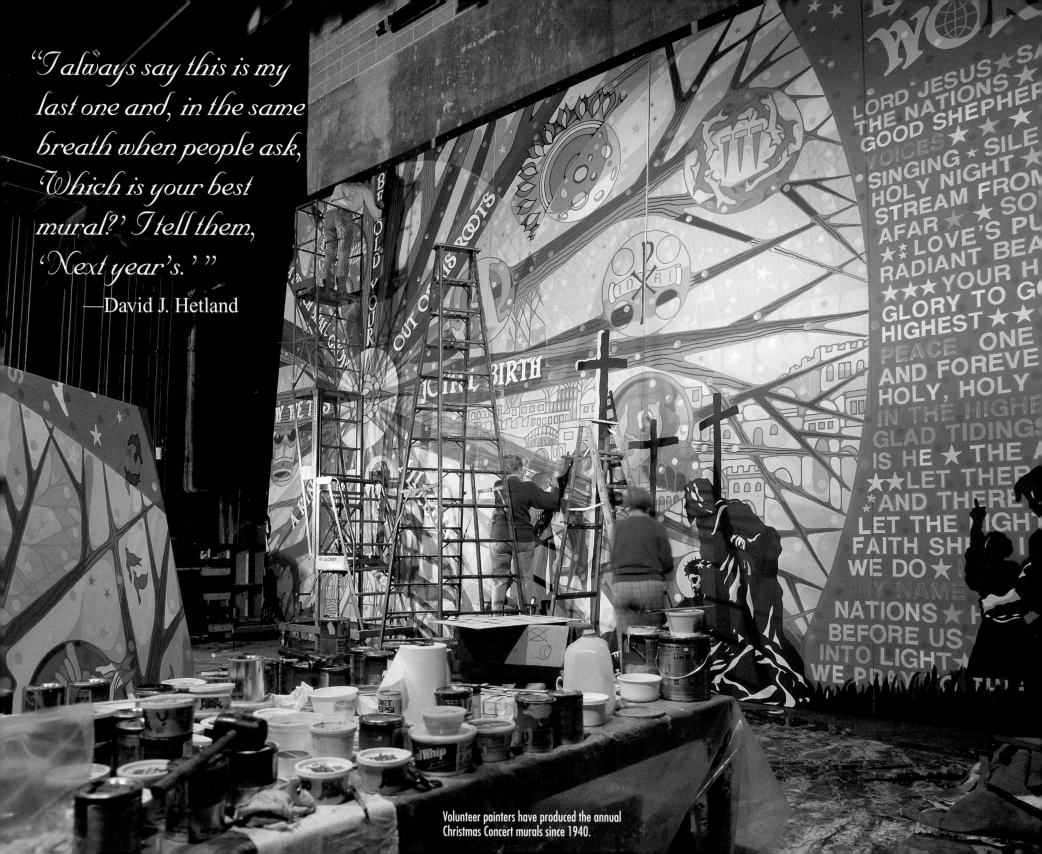

"I always say this is my last one and, in the same breath when people ask, 'Which is your best mural?' I tell them, 'Next year's.'"

—David J. Hetland

Volunteer painters have produced the annual Christmas Concert murals since 1940.

Chapter 4

IN THE IMAGE OF GOD

The Art

For most of the years that I have designed the Christmas murals – especially when we painted them in public areas like shopping malls – someone inevitably stops by to ask, "Where do you buy these patterns?"

*Rather than take offense, my facetious response is always the same: "From the Montgomery Ward catalog." That seems to satisfy the curious visitors, and my fellow painters all get a good chuckle out of it. But now I worry that my slight fabrication of the truth may have cast a gloomy shadow of suspicion upon the reputation of the entire effort. So I am compelled to set the record straight. Our patterns do **not** come from Montgomery Ward. They are ordered from the **Sears** catalog.*

A distinguishing hallmark of Concordia's Christmas Concerts has been their sensory approach to this worship experience. In addition to word and music, there is art. And, unlike that of many other Christmastime events, this art has evolved into something beyond mere decoration—it has become more than tinsel glistening on the tree. It is the visual word,

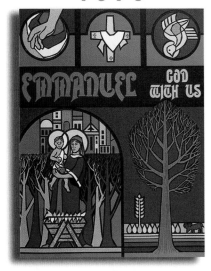

EMMANUEL, GOD WITH US

Conductors: Paul J. Christiansen
                Rodney Rothlisberger
                Russell Pesola
Narrators: George Schultz
                Helen Cermak

1979 mural

Cy Running brought artistic innovation to the Christmas Concert tradition.

activating another physical sense as we absorb intellectual substance and heartfelt experience.

Good liturgical art attempts to interpret and connect issues of faith and reality—in understandable terms. For the artist who conjures up these images from a place of conviction, the process becomes an act of faith. For the viewer who responds openly to such imagery, spiritual enlightenment blossoms.

A NEW VISION

By the time Paul Christiansen came to Concordia in 1937, the Music Club event had already established the tradition of a Christmas tableau. So it was not surprising that his first concert included a pantomimed Nativity scene with Mary at the manger surrounded by shepherds and an angel. The role of Mary was played by Imogene (Baker) Campbell '39, later elected the 1938 Homecoming queen. Carl Bailey '40 (who would later become chair of Concordia's physics department, academic dean and a dedicated Christmas mural painter) was a shepherd.

According to Eleanor Christiansen, "They didn't use a real baby, and I don't even remember if they used a doll. I think there was a light in the manger. Probably that year or the next year, they'd have some Christmas trees up in the chancel, and the choir would walk by and the trees would fall over."

In 1939 Donald Bentley volunteered ("I was chosen by the infamous Paul J. Christiansen 'stare' method") to help with the Christmas tableau:

> We used an empty piano carton which we "conned" from Stone Piano Company in Fargo. We cut out most of one side of the box and covered the opening with a sheet of white cloth. Behind that we set up the manger and positioned a flood light to silhouette the whole scene. We were quite pleased with the result, but were very happy to learn that Cy Running had been hired in the summer following and would be taking over the production and lighting for future concerts.
>
> It is almost embarrassing to look back and see how rudimentary our first attempt was. But I still believe that this effort was the original precursor to those wonderful galas that we see at Concordia now each year.

In the autumn of 1940 and at Paul Christiansen's suggestion, one of his former St. Olaf classmates, Cyrus M. Running, was hired to head Concordia's fledgling art department. (It was also a fortunate occurrence for me; decades later, Cy would become both my mentor and my friend.)

Professor Running and his wife Eldrid moved to Moorhead without ever having visited the campus. This was a good thing, he would later recall, because "nobody had decent equipment in those days, and if I had known what it was like, I may never have come."

Economically, times were tough in the early '40s. Running signed an annual contract for $1,800. He later

Cy Running began his teaching and mural-painting careers at Concordia in 1940.

recalled his first few months: "We came to town without any money, and I tried to get an advancement from the college but couldn't. If it hadn't been for people like a grocer named Clarence ('Andy') Anderson, we couldn't have made it. He let us charge groceries 'til we got our first check."

To supplement his meager salary, Running eventually began working for a local sign company in his spare time and during the summers. There, he gained some valuable experience: learning to work on a large scale. But he found painting signs to be uniformly uninspiring: "Terrible things. I hated them, but I did them. I had to paint these repulsively beautiful people with smiles, opening windows. And I did a whole series on Arco Coffee painted on the sides of buildings."

Christiansen was very excited by Running's presence in Moorhead, because he recognized the potential

of adding a more dynamic visual dimension to the Christmas Concerts: "I had grown up listening to meetings between Arne Flaten (chair of St. Olaf's art department), Oscar Overby (a St. Olaf music professor) and my father. They would plan the Christmas concerts at St. Olaf. And now, we had two minds to work on it here and two avenues of producing it—the visual as well as the music."

In his very first year, reported *The Concordian*, Running supervised the "decorations," which included "113 yards of blue sateen draped over the large archway in the center of the church (Trinity). Suspended against the dark cloth background was a single star. Two simulated art glass windows painted by the department on either side of the center arch depicted heavenly and earthly Christmas scenes." And, for the first time, a design by Running appeared on the program cover *(see page 20)*.

Along with Running, Erling Erickson '42 and Garland Lockrem '48 constituted "the department" referred to in *The Concordian* story. Erickson helped paint the two faux-stained-glass windows on butcher paper: "We oiled it up first (to render it translucent) and then went to work on it using oil paint. We did the entire project in three days, and Cy would say, 'Whomp it in!' I remember that we were so darned tired. Cy went home to bed, but I was in the choir. I don't even remember singing."

TAKING SHAPE

Following the 1941 concert at First Lutheran, Cy and Paul J. discussed the possibility of moving the event to the Moorhead Armory, which could seat more people and allow for more preparation and rehearsal time. Still, it was essentially a gymnasium—wrapped by a shallow balcony on three sides and a large proscenium stage on the fourth.

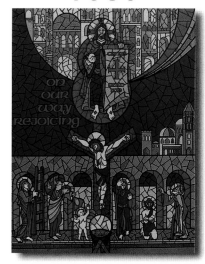

ON OUR WAY REJOICING

Conductors: Paul J. Christiansen
Rodney Rothlisberger
Russell Pesola
Narrator: George Schultz

O COME, ALL YE CHILDREN

Conductors:	Paul J. Christiansen
	Lowell Larson
	Russell Pesola
Narrator:	George Schultz

Sights and Sounds: A Collaborative Friendship

Paul Christiansen and Cy Running forged a lifelong friendship, and David Langseth '62 recounted an episode that aptly demonstrated the collegiality between the two men. As the choir rehearsed in the auditorium, Cy and numerous students were putting the finishing touches on the mural. Cy came over and stood by Paul J., watching his every move as he directed the choir. Paul J. noticed him watching, smiled, and stepped aside, inviting the art professor (and accomplished musician) to get on the podium and direct the choir: "He did, and with great seriousness picked up on the continuing number where Paul J. left off."

Both Cy and Paul used to tell the story of an early concert at the Moorhead Armory, when they had been working late to prepare for a concert. Tom Christenson '63 heard the story many times:

> During rehearsals, an ice storm had come through, completely glazing everything with almost an inch of ice. Paul's car doors were iced shut and, even after several efforts, could not be opened. Cy had ridden down to the Armory on his bicycle, which he luckily had parked inside the building. So, at one or two in the morning, the streets being solid ice, with Cy pedaling and Paul perched on the handlebars, they more or less "skated" home. The only thing that kept them upright, they said, was that they were singing a Bach two-part invention. Both claimed that they were convinced that if they had stopped singing, down they would have gone.

John Carlander '65 taught in Concordia's art department and had worked under Cy. Shortly

Both Paul Christiansen and Cy Running conducted Christmas Concert choirs during the war years. In addition to his strong art background, Running was known for his humor and musicality.

after Cy's death in 1976, Carlander decided he wanted to talk with Paul J. about it. His encounter showed him Paul's warmth:

> I just walked over to his house and knocked on his door. He came to the door, invited me in and we had a very good conversation about Cy and all the wonderful work that he had done over the years. Paul J. sat at one end of the room, smoking his pipe—I sat respectfully at the other end. I remember that he was upset about his grand piano, because it was going out of tune too often, and he referred to it as "that damned ox!" I was struck that day with Paul's human and warm side, and his sense of caring about Cy and the loss of a good colleague and friend.

Hop on—for a cozy ride home.

Acoustically, the new space was abominable. "It was out of necessity that we put a covering in the proscenium because so much of the sound went up," Running later recalled. "Then we got the idea, 'Why not paint something on there?' So that's how we started." Form followed function.

"It grew from year to year," said Christiansen, "and we felt that the three arts, really, the music and the visual art and the literature, should be combined to express ideas about Christmas."

And Ingrid, Paul's young daughter, looked forward to each new concert, hoping to find the Christmas star hidden in the painted backdrop. She once asked Running, "Will the star come again this year?"

He looked at her closely for a moment, then smiled reassuringly, "Yes, the star will come again."

"I never could see it," Ingrid recalled, "and then a spotlight would come on, and the star would shine— that was always a great moment for me."

BIGGER AND BETTER

With the move to Concordia's huge, newly constructed Memorial Auditorium in 1952, the need for continuing with an acoustical backdrop became even more prominent. Coincidentally, that year's was also the Silver Anniversary Christmas Concert, and it required three presentations, each seating 4,500 people happily jammed in elbow to elbow.

Flanked by 70 spruce trees, both risers and art were located at the base of the arching roof on the gym's north side, and the sound would faithfully follow the curve up and around and down again. Running would often lead friends to one particular place in the rickety wooden bleachers on the south end of the gym. "Here is where the sound is," he would assert. Though not the most comfortable seats in the house, they were always among the most coveted.

Growing up as a teenager in south Moorhead and having his father working as a Concordia steam engineer, young Tom Christenson gradually became familiar with both the college and its personalities. One late-November evening, he was crossing the campus amid the season's first snowfall:

An arched ceiling helped direct the sound out and over the audience from the choir risers at one end of Memorial Auditorium.

I heard delightful music coming through an open window in the art barn. I thought that the music perfectly fit the falling snow and the mood of the evening. I went in to find Cy Running working on a large drawing, to which he was adding detail and Scotch-taping colored paint chips. Soon enough, I recognized that it was the cartoon (full-scale pattern) for the Christmas Concert set.

It didn't take long before Cy asked me if I

LEAD ON, O KING ETERNAL

Concordia student David Berg chosen to narrate concert

Conductors: Paul J. Christiansen
               Lowell Larson
               Russell Pesola
Narrators: David Berg
               Nancy O'Leary

wanted to help paint it. "Sure," I said, "how much does it pay?"

He laughed and said, "I'll see that you get twice what I get."

I understood the point of this phrase and asked, "Where do I sign up, and when do we begin?"

"Over in the gym, tomorrow afternoon. I'll bring supper for you in a bag. It's only fair—I don't know if you can paint, and you don't know if I can cook."

Many long evenings were spent painting. In the early years, this was done in North Hall, originally constructed in 1893 as Clay County and Moorhead's first hospital. Upon acquisition by the college, it later housed the music and art departments.

Those laborious evening sessions stretched into long nights as the concert drew near. Because the Moorhead Armory hosted Saturday night dances, Christiansen and Running, along with their choirs and

Super-Sizing the Art: Then and Now

Historically, one of the greatest challenges in producing the Christmas Concert art was the process used to transfer the small, original drawing to the large muslin panels for painting. Until 1978, the technique used was a combination of *scaling* and *gridding*, and it demanded some artistic skill. This arduous and often imprecise operation involved actually locating key points on the drawing, such as an elbow and a wrist, and measuring them with an architectural scale. These points were then repositioned on the larger-scale panels and connected with charcoal lines. It often took a full week to complete the transfer.

Currently, a *projection* system using high-contrast negative slides allows rapid and accurate transfers of even the most complex and challenging art. With unskilled volunteer assistance, it is now possible to complete the entire process in a single day.

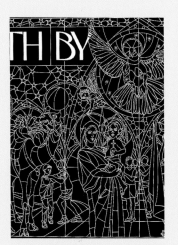

High-contrast slide

Projection transfer

Finished mural detail

crews, often could not begin setup or touch-up work until after midnight for the next day's concert. With the completion of Memorial Auditorium in 1951, the entire painting project was moved there—behind the west bleachers on a dirt floor.

In addition to creating a name for himself as an artist, Running also developed a reputation as a musician and humorist. He combined his talents in a parody he called "I Hate Music," which he publicly performed for civic, church and college groups for many years. Among his students and faculty colleagues, Running was known as a comic—especially while working so intensely in the Field House on the annual Christmas Concert art.

Tom Christenson recounted one such memorable experience there with Cy:

I was the guy who never knew when to quit or go home. So frequently, Cy and I would be the last ones working on the set into the wee hours of the morning. At about 2:30 a.m., Cy took a break from painting and went over to the grand piano that had been used for an earlier rehearsal.

He began playing boogie-woogie and ragtime pieces that he knew. A few minutes later, we heard someone shouting. There, in the north balcony, stood Albert Paranto in his pajamas. Albert was the building's janitor who, we discovered, slept in the little windowless room off the north balcony.

Cy Running always added finishing touches to each Christmas mural—day or night, no matter the height.

The raucous piano playing woke him up, and he came forth to vent his displeasure.

Cy shouted up to him, "Albert, as long as you're up, come on down here." Albert did as he was requested and toddled barefoot down to the piano.

"I'm sorry I woke you up, but this gives me a chance to sing the special song I wrote for you." At that point, Cy broke into a piano-accompanied vocal piece, singing three verses of a well-rhymed country-style tune. The chorus to each verse began, "Albert, dear Albert, the king of the Field House . . . ."

Albert was genuinely touched by it and forgave Cy for waking him up. As he padded off to bed, he turned to say, "When you guys get done with the big stuff, call me and I'll come down with my fine brush to put on the finishing touches."

Nothing was ready until Cy sat at the piano, said Casey Jones. "When everything was all set and the artwork was done, Cy would sit down and play some jazz on the piano. Then we knew that it was done."

Philip Thompson '55 witnessed another of Running's performances: "When all of the painting was completed, Cy was standing on top of the 30-foot scaffold and announced with great exuberance that the job was finished. He then proceeded to do a spiral-slide down to the floor on the outside leg of the scaffold in the matter of a few seconds." In later years, these acrobatics

**BEHOLD, MY SERVANT
WHOM I UPHOLD**

*Moorhead concert expanded to
four performances*

Conductors:	Paul J. Christiansen
	Lowell Larson
	Russell Pesola
Narrator:	David Berg

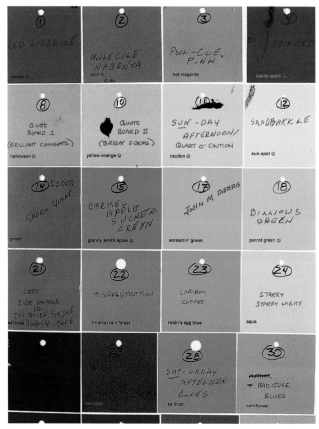

Numbered color charts have guided volunteer painters for decades. In more recent years, whimsical names for the colors have also occasionally been bestowed.

were often accompanied by either a deafening whistle or a few bars of some glitzy pop tune.

From the very beginning, Running involved his art students and departmental colleagues in the Christmas painting project. Kay (Ornberg) Jensen '62 remembered Cy saving her small parts of the mural to finish during studio time so that she could participate during the busy Christmas season, when she had a part-time job.

Because of its scale and the limited number of days set aside to complete the work, Cy began formulating a system whereby volunteers could come and go, according to their individual schedules, and still be productive. It became known as the paint-by-letter system and involved assigning each can of paint a letter of the alphabet. These corresponded to spaces needing paint on the design that had been drawn in charcoal. Painters, for example, simply grabbed the can marked "C" and filled in all of the "C" spaces on the canvas. The process continues to this day, though now as the more pedestrian paint-by-*number* system, since we eventually had more colors than available letters.

To his sometimes skeptical students in subsequent years, Cy would often claim to have been the inventor of the paint-by-number system. Research seems to indicate that he was correct. The first commercial paint-by-number set was apparently marketed by the Palmer Paint Company in 1952, more than a decade *after* Cy developed the very same process for the Concordia Christmas Concert art.

For the 1953-54 academic year, Running was granted a sabbatical leave. He and his entire family went south of the border, "not to be exotic, but because that was the only place we could live on half-salary. So all six of us in a Studebaker Champion—you know, the 'gutless wonder,' 85-horse and a rack on top—headed

Art students were always involved in banner and mural painting for the concerts.

for Mexico. And, for the first time, I was able to paint every day, all the time."

In his absence, Elizabeth Strand '46 assumed responsibility for the Christmas Concert mural. By then a Concordia art faculty member, she had been a freshman in 1942 and had worked on the sets at the Moorhead Armory. Now she was in charge of the project, an experience she described as providing "moments of total frustration as well as great anticipation and hilarity."

Another art department member, Dean Bowman,

Elizabeth Strand worked on murals as a student and later instructor.

Dean Bowman assisted with painting and designed the 1967 mural in Cy Running's absence.

came to Concordia in 1957 and often assisted with the Christmas mural. Norman Holen '59 filled in during the 1963-64 academic year, with Bowman on sabbatical.

Holen volunteered to help Cy Running with the lettering that ran nearly the entire length of Memorial Auditorium. As Running left one day to go back to his teaching, he reminded Holen to watch for spelling errors. Holen remembered, "While I was painting, a student came into the building to say that my wife had called and that I had an emergency at home. After working on the plumbing, I went back to the gym and continued painting without my mind on the project. I missed Cy's only misspelled word, of course, and he had to reletter a large section of the huge banner."

A decade later, with Running again on leave, this time in Europe, it fell to Dean Bowman to design the 1967 Christmas Concert mural. Before he left, Running appointed me to be the student chair of the mural committee, responsible for assisting the designer and recruiting adequate student help.

Bowman's design consisted of seven completely independent images separated by spaces into which translucent, colored-plastic rectangles were affixed. Painters worked from a full-color rendering *(see page 51)* using latex paint with such exotic names as "Garden Party." And, not to be overshadowed by Running's musical ability, Bowman spontaneously went to the north balcony of the Field House, erupted into a lively, loud operatic aria and began waving his arms emphatically. It was long after midnight, and we painters were more than startled. In later years, he would reluctantly confess to being "musically challenged."

Almost immediately following the Moorhead concerts (in a letter dated December 14, 1967), Bowman wrote to the Runnings, "Somewhere in Europe":

Dear Cy and Eldrid:
Sorry not to have written sooner, but I have been busy.
The letter you wrote from Amsterdam and apparently mailed on September 26, reached me on November 5th. It was all marked up with all sorts of irritated stampings. Apparently Europeans do not like mail emanating from their shores with U.S. Airmail stamps and envelopes.
Well, the Christmas Concert is over and it went fairly well. I didn't estimate the glitter and cotton too well so there are several 5-lb. bags of assorted colors left over. I suppose you'll find a use for them next year. It worked fine for the snow effect in the finale while the little kids in their snowsuits were on stage. About half a bale of cotton left. Used it for stuffing on the 18-ft. Santa Claus. Soft sculpture, you know. The very latest thing. He was suspended ("hung" is a better word) out in front of the Field House over the entrance canopy. He looked good until he got thoroughly soaked in the light drizzle we had on opening day. Then he sort of

I HAVE COME A LIGHT INTO THE WORLD

Conductors:	Paul J. Christiansen
	Lowell Larson
	Russell Pesola
Narrator:	David Berg

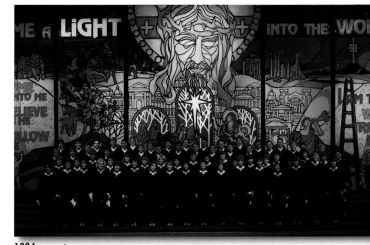

1984 concert

I AM THE GOOD SHEPHERD

Paul J. Christiansen's final Christmas Concert before retiring in 1986

First major television broadcast of Christmas Concerts

Conductors:	Paul J. Christiansen
	Lowell Larson
	Russell Pesola
Narrators:	Peter Halverson
	Julie Limoseth

drooped. Even the half-pound of sequins sewed in each eye failed to raise a twinkle. The paint ran on his rosy cheeks and red nose. (I didn't know acrylics would do that.) If I were to do it again, I would use vinyl; the muslin is just too fragile for really monumental things.

But a lot of people thought it was a start for better things to come. The high point of the evening came when the audience stood and sang "White Christmas." You know, the beautiful song by Irv Berlin. As the song ended, hats were thrown into the air. A lot of people wept. During the melee that followed, a choir member was hit over the eye by a chair. It was such an emotional experience that the last two nights of the concert were canceled. People just couldn't take it.

In regard to your urgent letter—that took a month—you needn't have worried so much. You left quite complete notes and recipes. There were no difficulties other than those I made for myself. I had good help from all and a lot of help from a few, and that's the way it has to be.

The Field House is quite a place. After getting the panels out, I rather missed the freedom of the dirt floor and the sense of security. The panels make a fairly private world penetrated by an occasional visitor who braved my baleful stares and the constant threat of a shower from a brush being rinsed out. And, of course, the "sounds" got through.

1985 concert

I think somebody should write a symphony on a "Day in the Field House." The initial movement is brisk with calisthenics and Joan Hult's punctuations; then a slow, cathedral flavor for Chapel. The afternoon has a big beat with the modern dancers, followed by the raucous Sonny Gulsvig whipping his team into shape. The final movement is the tumultuous cacophony of a real ball game. When *that*

noise funnels down behind the bleachers, it is really something else.

Merry Christmas from all of us here. All best—
Dean

CHANGING OF THE GUARD

In the summer of 1972, Paul Christiansen called a choir board meeting at his cabin on Bad Medicine Lake for the purpose of discussing the art transition. Ill health finally ended Cy's tenure both in the art department and on the Christmas Concert project. His thirtieth and final mural was designed for that year's concert, but it fell to Charles Beck '48 to complete the painting. Beck was one of Running's early students and had become a well-known artist and teacher.

Notes from Running to Beck on the mural design included color selections and the notation, "When in doubt, wing it!"

Cy and Eldrid Running subsequently met with James Cermak, a new member of the speech and theater department faculty, to solicit his assistance. "This is a fairly simple project," Running told Cermak that afternoon at coffee. "No, it wasn't," laughed Cermak. "It was a massive project that he had carried on for so many years. I wasn't qualified to do the design, but I promised that I would continue to help with the technical arrangements, including the lighting."

It fell to Paul Allen '62, who was subsequently hired as Running's replacement on the art faculty, to head the Christmas Concert project. As a former Concordia art student and a veteran of the mural-painting project under Running, Allen had the necessary experience. He had also sung in the concerts as a student and so brought a multidisciplinary dimension to his responsibilities.

"To conceive of being in a leadership position to do that was kind of a mind-bender," he recalled, "but I

Cyrus M. Running designed Christmas Concert art from 1940 through 1972.

FROM EVERLASTING TO EVERLASTING

Declining health ended Cy Running's Christmas Concert tenure with this mural (inset) designed in 1972. At right are details from the design and completed mural, painted by Charles Beck, one of Running's early students.

GO FORTH IN PEACE

René Clausen's first year as conductor of Concordia Choir

Full orchestra added to concert

Conductors: René Clausen
Erik Christiansen
J. Robert Hanson
Narrator: Peter Halverson

Erik Christiansen both sang and served as an assistant conductor under his father.

just tried to remember everything I could, and we went about it."

In Allen's student days, the mural was painted in the Field House, on the dirt floor behind the portable wooden bleachers. By the time he returned to head the project, the Frances Frazier Comstock The-atre building had been constructed, and the painting was done there in the scene shop, in the Lab Theatre or on the main stage. It was a great improvement, and it also provided a closer prox-imity to Jim Cermak's technical counsel and expertise. Sometimes, under Cermak's super-vision, theatre students built and base-painted concert flats to be used for the mural.

Paul Allen replaced Cy Running in the art department and designed murals from 1973 through 1977.

"For Paul, there was nothing more important than the art. He was so intensely involved," Cermak observed. On one occasion, for example, Allen came close to finishing his painting *during* the opening con-cert. "I was using a pointillistic technique, little dots," he explained. "There were mountains and they shifted from a tan to a purple and we had a lot of different val-ues of these colors in order to get them to blend right.

"We were right down to the wire," he laughed, "and I remember that after the dress rehearsal, it was work harder and harder and harder to finish. And then there was no heat in the Field House because they were trying to cool it off for the concerts. I had to wear gloves. It was getting to be six o'clock on the night of the opening concert and Kurt Wycisk said to Betty

Strand, 'What are we gonna do?' I got it finished in about 15 minutes, and we got everything down and away and the whole thing was done. But that was a really complex one."

Strand and Dean Bowman also returned to col-laborate with Allen on the Christmas art. They and several students lettered massive banners, some of which topped the wooden bleachers while others were suspended in various locations around Memorial Audi-torium. "Those letters were at least three feet tall, and they were on a big roll," Allen recalled. "Betty had to

Full-color renderings (above) were routinely executed during Paul Allen's Christmas mural tenure. A pointillistic painting technique (right) required many long and patient hours.

roll it out and craft the letters from a precise sketch. I don't think she was able to see the whole thing until it

Concordia art instructor Betty Strand often assisted with the Christmas mural and banner lettering.

was put up because she did one section at a time." And Bowman used a four-inch brush to create his single-stroke "Concordia Gothic" lettering style.

Resembling colorful Christmas cards, the printed program covers have been the responsibility of the mural designer. They are designed to reflect the annual themes of the concerts and are intended to be taken home as a durable keepsake of the Christmas Concert worship experience.

Programs, too, have evolved—from early mimeographed stencils to full-color offset reproduction. Some of the changes that occurred were not made by choice, but by mandate. During World War II, for example, the programs went from black and colored inks to blue-only *(see page 22)* because the metallic content in some inks was needed for the war-materials effort. When peace was finally achieved, all colors of ink returned to the covers once again.

Many singers and instrumentalists remember being handed copies of new arrangements and revised interludes "still hot" from the ditto machine. Paul Christiansen's penchant for last-minute changes to both music and text affected the printed Christmas Concert programs. Don Aasland, foreman at Diercks Printing in Moorhead for many years, also recalled handling some hot copy: "Paul J. would always come down to the shop with a longhand version of the entire program. He used a stubby pencil and it was always dull," Aasland laughed, "so I'd make him stand there while I read every word back to him. He didn't have much patience. And there was always a bargaining that went on: 'When can I make the last changes?' Paul would want to know. Then I would go over to his

LIGHT ETERNAL, LIGHT OF THE WORLD

Conductors:	René Clausen
	Christopher Cock
	J. Robert Hanson
Narrator:	Peter Halverson

Wholesale program changes were not uncommon during the Christiansen years.

house and sit there while he gassed me out with his pipe while reading the final proof."

As an undergraduate art student in the late '60s, I can vividly remember wishing that someday I might be able to design *just one* Christmas Concert mural—for the experience. In retrospect, it reminds me of how my young daughter justified one of her first trick-or-treat outings on Halloween—she went "for the exercise, not for the candy."

When Paul Allen announced his retirement from the project after the 1977 concert, Paul Christiansen asked me to take it over. By this time, I had been a full-time Concordia staff member for four years, serving as director of communications. The thought of adding a project of this magnitude was only slightly more than

Generations of Volunteer Painters

My daughter, Kristen Hetland '00 (left), was our youngest painter. She wielded her brush on the mural at the age of three. Carl Bailey (right) has been one of our painting stalwarts—at eighty-something, he's still going strong.

fiercely ridiculous—and intimidating. But then, a wonderful thing happened. Dean Bowman, whom I had assisted on the 1967 mural, came to me with an offer to even the score: if I would design and supervise

David Hetland (left) and Dean Bowman consulted on 1989 mural touch-up.

the project, he would be responsible for all of the painting. Wow! With a commitment of support like that, how could I refuse? So I didn't.

Cy once told me that the Christmas Concert mural should be "poster art," to provide an ephemeral, for-the-moment experience. I must be doing it right, because I have become the master of disposable art that is,

I always say, best when viewed in the dark and from a great distance. Each year, I facetiously remind the choral conductors that people have surely come for the art, and that I am grateful for their best musical efforts to enhance the experience for the audience.

As it has developed, my design process takes place every day of the year. Even before I have a theme or any of the text or music, I am planning. What should be the mood this year? Should it be done in a particular style? How about the color palette?

These questions I mull over and over each hot summer, as I follow my mower row by row around the yard. Sometimes I have wondrous insights, but mostly not. Still, I have fun drawing imaginary pictures that are usually forgotten in deference to a good idea, then a better one and yet another. Every square of tile in my morning shower becomes a section of the forthcoming Christmas panel, and holiday music can be heard in my studio throughout much of the year.

With autumn's crisp chill, sleep is often interrupted

Mural research is begun in early summer, and the subsequent design process often takes a full month in the fall to complete before painting can begin.

by inspiration—perhaps fueled by desperation. With paper and pen within easy reach, I am prepared to accept a stroke of brilliance at any hour and to record same. In the morning, my notepad is often full of wondrous scribblings but, as with my summer dreaming, it soon becomes apparent that the light was not on.

Actually, many of my mural designs begin as "napkin art." It is not uncommon for me to be describing the upcoming year's theme to a lunch partner, then quickly sketch a possible visual approach to help make it more clear. These are often the seed from which the finished art grows. Once the final scale drawing is begun, I take it to bed with me, placing it upright against a nearby dresser so that it becomes the last thing I see at night and the first thing I see in the morning. This may go on for several weeks until the work is finally finished.

Early in my tenure, I learned the importance of trying to make each year's painting both better than and, especially, *different* from previous efforts. These objectives were the result of a Monday evening rehearsal, when the mural had been set in place only hours earlier. Students were strolling in—looking at the art for the first time and, I naively thought, being thoroughly impressed. Then two young women walked directly past me. One, obviously a freshman, looked up at the mural and exclaimed, "Wow!" The other, apparently with upperclass experience, casually glanced up and replied, "Oh, yeah, they put *that* thing up every year."

BLUE DOGS, PURPLE CAMELS

One of my favorite quotes comes from the writer Doris Lessing: "Any human anywhere will blossom into a hundred unexpected talents and capacities simply

David Hetland's rough napkin sketches (top) often find their way onto finished Christmas murals (bottom).

by being given the opportunity to do so."

That statement is no more true than for the scores of volunteer painters who annually brave winter's chill and icy roads to become a part of the Christmas Concert experience. With them come the diversities of age and gender, experience and interest, profession and faith. What binds them together is the chance to work briefly on this project and with each other.

On my watch, three couples have been among the most dedicated painters: Carl and June '43 Bailey, Dean and Lois Bowman and Ames and May Bredeson. They appeared nearly every evening and weekend that we worked over a several-decade period. Because their last names all begin with the same letter, they were affectionately dubbed the "B-Squad."

Each of them brought some special gifts, and a few peculiarities, to our project. Carl, for example, has insisted on painting spaces of any size with a three-quar-

Liturgical Art Laboratory

At times, the Christmas Concert mural serves as a sort of experiment for commissioned liturgical artwork. It's the only environment I've found that allows me to create art on such a large scale.

In 1989, I used the mural with the theme "O Come, O Come, Emmanuel" to test preliminary images for a huge stained-glass window project for the Christian Life Center at Trinity Lutheran Church in Moorhead. (The old church was also the site of many early Christmas Concerts.)

Images, including the dove, nautilus shell, stars and planets, and hands holding a cross, all appear in the mural design (top), completed mural (bottom left) and, finally, in the finished Trinity window.

ter-inch brush. June stakes out her claim on a particular panel and defends her territory with great vigor—and never fails to question whether I *really* want blue dogs and purple camels. (I do!) Dean always figured that

"B-Squad" members Dean and Lois Bowman (top) and Ames and May Bredeson

one coat of paint was good enough; Lois knew that there would be at least three. Ames was our "Waterboy" (fetching buckets of clean water in a small red wagon) until his passing, too soon, in 1993. May brings home-made cookies for birthdays or for any reason whatso-ever. Individually, they have painted. Collectively, they have become a personal treasure.

As a staunch concert goer, June Bailey has often overheard erroneous comments made by other nearby audience members and is never content to let them go unchallenged. Once, a man seated next to her insisted that the mural was lighted from behind because of its

stained-glass glow. This, she firmly pointed out, was impossible because the panels were flush to the opaque, permanent, metal bleachers of the Field House. On another occasion, someone was upset that the painters hadn't removed a ladder from in front of the mural. Actually, the ladder was painted *on* the mural to represent an instrument of Christ's passion. It would be safe to assume that this misconception was soon corrected.

Dean Bowman was the only "trained" artist in the bunch. Having long ago retired from Concordia's art department and even longer ago repaid the "debt" he thought he owed me for my meager help on his 1967 mural design, it was finally time for him to call it quits. A growing demand for his own work and a pair of aching knees led to his retire-ment from the Christmas project following the 1991 Christmas Concert.

In his place, Bowman recommended Karen Stensrud '85, a freelance writer and former art minor. She had spent several years assisting with the painting and lettering. Now, as my right hand on the project, she protects her textual

"B-Squad" member June Bailey (above right) clears up audience misconceptions she overhears during concerts.

Former Concordia academic dean, physics department chair and "B-Squad" member Carl Bailey prepared this Paint Weight Study (right) in response to a casual, late-evening question.

Ames "Waterboy" Bredeson (above) took good care of the painters.

Paint weight study   16 Nov. 1991

From two trials on a test surface, the dry weight of paint, per coat, is 0.022 lbs per square foot, within an accuracy limit of about ± 10%.

The panel area:

$$(8 \times 20 \times 7) + (12 \times 16 \times 7) = 2,460 \text{ square feet}$$

ignoring the painted edges which would add about an additional 55 square feet or so.

So the total paint weight, per coat, is (dry)

$$\left(.022 \frac{lbs}{ft^2}\right)(2,460 \, ft^2) = 54 \, lbs \pm 10\%.$$

If two coats are applied, the total paint weight (dry) is about 108 lbs ± 10%.

[i.e., 54/20 = 2.7 lbs per panel per coat.]

As a check: the weight of wet paint is about 11 lbs/gal. On drying, the weight falls to about 61%; that is, the dry weight is 6.7 lbs/gal.

If 108 lbs (dry weight) were applied, we used

$$\frac{108 \, lbs}{6.7 \, lbs/gal} = 16.1 \text{ gallons}$$

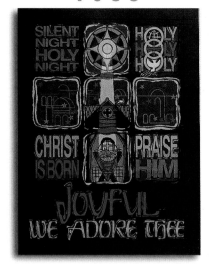

JOYFUL WE ADORE THEE

Second nationally televised broadcast

Conductors:	René Clausen
	Christopher Cock
	J. Robert Hanson
Narrator:	Peter Halverson

1988 concert

turf by drawing charcoal outlines about four inches around each letter as a warning to others not to trespass. "I've developed sort of a nasty reputation about that," she admitted.

Because of her slight build, Karen is assigned the careful job of matching the design elements at each seam. When painting has progressed to a suitable point, the panels are laid on the floor and snugged up against each other. Then, in stocking feet, Karen delicately tip-toes out on the "balance beam," crouches and connects the lines across the joints. Even a slight slip would result in falling through the stretched muslin. This process saves an immense amount of difficult work, because when the panels are finally erected in the Field House, they can only be reached from scaffolds or hydraulic lifts.

Soliciting painters is an annual task. Because I am not a member of the art faculty as were my predecessors, I do not have immediate access to the pool of art students. And so, the recruitment process must be a little more vigorous and varied. Usually this includes a news release that is distributed to local and regional media, detailing the location, dates and times for painting. *The* (Fargo) *Forum* takes the prize, though, for its succinct headline one year: "Have huge mural, need many painters."

In one of my first years of designing the mural, I asked Paul J. if he would announce our painting

Murals

Mural painting assistant Karen Stensrud is also a poet. She penned these lines in 1994 to evoke the design for that year's Christmas Concert mural:

Sketch hands, old and young, to cover canvas, smoothe soft curves that make a face, a daughter, a Christ.

Brush in trees, star shadows, imagine color where I cannot. Paint divine cities dancing in golden crowns.

Balance scale and answers. Mix joy with bright hues. Weave laughter into textures— soft as whispered prayers, sharp as kyrie.

schedule to the choirs, because I needed some help. Notorious for his tart rejoinders, his simple response to me was, "Singers sing and painters paint."

I took that as a firm "No!"

In contrast, when Gordon Moe was student manager of The Concordia Choir, he staged a competition between sections to see which of them could accumulate the greatest number of painting hours. A hot tub-homemade pizza party hosted by René Clausen at his home was the prize for the paint-splashing altos.

Long distance: Kathy Buck, from the Seattle area, takes the prize for distance traveled to volunteer. Almost every year, she flies to Fargo and paints for a week.

Every year, it seems, passersby and painters ask, "What happens to the murals after the concerts?" I used to take perverse delight in telling people that they were "destroyed," because it caused such consternation. Then, to be more politically correct, I would say that we "recycled" them. The truth is that we paint over them once or twice, before they become dropcloths for succeeding years.

Then there are the annual calls from churches and individuals who either want to install the murals permanently in their sanctuaries or glue them to their garage doors as seasonal decoration. Churches realize neither the immense scale of the panels nor their impermanence—that they are only temporary and are intended to be viewed from a considerable distance. As for the garage door application, I say, "Gee, I wish I could help you, but we use *interior* latex paint and it will not withstand our harsh winter weather." What I really mean by that is, "It just ain't never gonna happen." Christmas

Notably Quotable

Kristin Kuehl '92 began working on the Christmas murals while still an art major at Concordia. Based upon her experience as a summer Bible camp counselor, she introduced the "Quote Board" to the painting venue. It was a large sheet of paper upon which interesting, funny comments made by other painters were recorded.

Often these entries were taken out of context or resulted from fatigue at the end of a long day. They appear here unattributed, but the actual Quote Board boldly lists the author—frequently to his or her great embarrassment:

"There isn't anything you can mess up tonight that you can't fix tomorrow night."

"You know, this paint is going to cast a shadow—there are so many layers."

Rookie painter: "What shall I do?"
Senior painter: "Go where I have been and fix what I have dripped."

Proud painter: "How does it look?" *Head painter:* "Great, in the dark."

"This black paint smells like cows' breath! And I've had cows breathe on me before."

"It's Day Two and you're starting to bug me."

"Are these lines supposed to help us?"

"I love it when you don't have to be careful when you paint."

'I really miss that messy thing we did last year."

"You designed this? You must have a *big* brain!"

Kris Kuehl, a faithful painter, originated the "Quote Board."

"I'm forced to tell you—that looks good."

"Anyone who would paint a camel purple is nuts!"

Lowly painter: "Which are the leaves?" *Head painter:* "The green things."

Concert murals, like the music, are really intended to be transitory—for the moment. Afterwards, they will, it is hoped, live on in memory and spirit.

One of the most remarkable characteristics of the Christmas Concerts through the years has been their consistent ability to achieve interdisciplinary relationships and harmony—word to music, music to art, art to technical production, technical production to word and music. Those relationships can only be described as *synergistic*: the final outcome is more than the sum of its individual components. And that is powerful stuff.

This synergistic effort—one in which every person who sings or plays a note, wields a paintbrush, pounds a nail, hangs a light or adjusts a sound mixer—is

Borrowed painting space in a shopping mall often meant sharing the area with other events such as pigeon shows and radio-controlled car races.

Art Preservation

Because the annual Christmas Concert murals are unceremoniously "recycled" each year, Laura Nelson '99 undertook a preservation project of her own. As a member of the Freshman Choir and later the Chapel Choir, she began replicating the murals "to keep them alive."

Carefully freehanding each design from a photograph, she used bedsheets as her canvas and applied acrylic paint to them. Each creation required more than 40 hours of work.

"You can't imagine all of the color combinations," she observed.

Laura Nelson painted miniature murals during each of her four years as a Concordia student.

something each of us tries not to take for granted. Art has become but one of the traditional elements to develop over the 75-year history of the Christmas Concerts. But working with others to create something greater than any of us, than all of us, is the true blessing of this experience.

As a student manager, Gordon Moe organized a painting competition among choir sections. He would later become the full-time manager of musical organizations at Concordia.

How are traditions like this born? I think I know. Several years ago, I asked to have the Christmas risers and mural set two feet farther forward from their customary location to provide a better line of sight for audience members. But I was told that it would not be possible to make such a change. When I asked why, the answer was, "Because it's tradition—we always do it this way." So I went to Jim Cermak, technical director, told him what had transpired and asked if he could intervene on my behalf. He said, "Sure, no problem." With that, he ripped up the piece of masking tape that indicated the position of the risers and moved it forward two feet. "There," he asserted, "now next year it will be a tradition."

A Touch of Whimsy

We usually tend to take issues related to our faith pretty seriously, and that is usually appropriate. But, as someone has suggested, if you don't think God has a

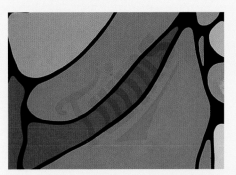

sense of humor, take a look at an ostrich.

It has become widely known that the Christmas Concert artwork often contains a subtle, whimsical element done, originally, to attract and amuse the volunteer painters. When this practice began for certain is unknown, but Erling Erickson recounted a trick he and Garland Lockrem played on Cy Running in 1940, his first year. "While he was gone, we painted a crack in the panel to look like a rip. It was about three inches wide by four inches high—and he believed it!"

More recent efforts have included a Minnesota Twins logo in 1988 (when the team won the World Series), a planet in the form of a basketball in 1995 (when my daughter's high school team won the state tournament), Calvin and Hobbes in 1989 (simply because Dean Bowman liked these comic strip characters), treebark that read "NAFTA—uffda" in 1994, a craft resembling Noah's ark but inscribed with the name *USS F-M* in 1997 (to commemorate that spring's terrible flooding) and a star in the sky

dubbed "Kenneth" in 1998 (referring to the independent counsel then prosecuting President Clinton). But the best known "secret" was hidden in the 1988 mural. It was a presidential election year, and way down low, under the blue camel, there appeared a quail under a bush (yes, to suggest Dan and George).

Lighting changes were all pre-programmed and computer-driven but had to be manually cued for 1997's televised concert.

Chapter 5

LET THERE BE LIGHT

The Production

It is too bad lighting effects could not be used more freely for this annual event. With a bit longer preparation the program could easily become one of the best-known and attended music events in the two cities. That is a goal at which to aim.

—*The Concordian,* December 15, 1938

It was true that, in the earliest days of the concerts, a wide gap separated lofty vision and technical reality. After the 1938 Christmas Radio Party, Concordia radio host G. Lydian Schoberg reported one noticeable technical error: "The mobile short-wave microphone wire only reached as far as one of the fir trees on the lawn instead of into (President Brown's) house, when operators rushed from car to Dr. Brown's residence. But that isn't the hardest problem that the president of Concordia had to solve . . . and before you had even noticed it on the air, he was out without coat or

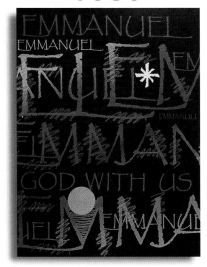

EMMANUEL, GOD WITH US

Conductors: René Clausen
                         Christopher Cock
                         J. Robert Hanson
Narrator: Peter Halverson

hat in 20-below weather to read his greeting to you by the light of a flashlight."

With steady and determined effort, modest technical improvements were made and were gradually woven into the fabric of the concert. Arthur Sanden, science instructor and superintendent of buildings and grounds from 1943 to 1966, became the man in charge of concert lighting.

Assisted in 1946 by Roger Sanders '48 and Russell Halaas '52, Professor Sanden faced the challenge of how to light the concert effectively with but a single homemade rheostat. "We had two cues," Halaas chuckled. "We had to light the star and then the baby Jesus. We turned the dimmer up and then brought it down again."

As an eight-year-old, Tom Christenson sat in the Armory's balcony that evening with his parents, awestruck by the art:

> The painted backdrop represented the city of Bethlehem, dark against a deep blue, star-filled sky. As the auditorium darkened toward the end, I remember the star and the manger glowing with what seemed to be an inner light. This made a great aesthetic impression on me, and it sparked a technical curiosity. How did they make those things glow like that?
>
> Immediately after the concert, I tore away from my folks and ran up to the front to take a closer look. Behind the large painted flats, I saw a round-faced man (who I would later know was Cy Running).
>
> He turned in my direction, looked over the top of his glasses and said, "Well, what do you think?"
>
> I responded, "How did you do that?"
>
> He called me over and showed me the homemade water-bucket transformer that allowed the lights to be turned up and down gradually. He also pointed out the spots he had oiled on the canvas backdrop to allow light to glow through from behind.
>
> At that point, my parents found me and began to apologize for the bother I was, but Cy said, "No bother. Every night hundreds of people see this thing, but he's the first one to come back and ask how it works."
>
> This was my introduction to the behind-the-scenes workings of the Christmas Concerts. I had no idea then that Cy and I would someday spend

Performed for an audience of 6,700 people, the 1950 concert featured a traditional Nativity scene set in a contemporary village.

> countless hours together working on sets and the lights for them, nor that I would someday end up developing some lighting tricks of my own.

And so he would. While yet a high school student, Christenson became a fixture in Concordia's theatre program. He and his friend David Dussere '61 would often spend their evenings building sets and hanging lights from the traps in the ceiling of Old Main's auditorium. In 1957, the pair collaborated on installing Christmas Concert lighting and took turns running it. Then, for the next five years, Christenson assumed full responsibility for the lighting.

Working on any technical arrangements in Concordia's Field House has never been a simple task—in fact, sometimes it was downright scary, according to Christenson. "To hang lights, first we had to put the aluminum scaffolding all the way up to the ceiling," he recounted. "Though it looked sturdy enough from the floor, even with

Tom Christenson began his Christmas Concert association at an early age.

four or five sections on it, the whole thing would begin to groan and lean considerably as we pulled additional sections up on a rope." Then began the arduous task of carefully hoisting chains, clamps, pipes and lighting instruments up the same way.

When it was all over, the process was reversed:

One night after the final concert, I went home early with the flu—thinking that I could come back the next day to disassemble everything. But at about midnight, I got a call from Don Krause '57 who, at that time, was the Field House manager. He said, "We need all of the equipment cleared from the building tonight because there's a wrestling tournament beginning here tomorrow. I've got several of my boys working tonight, but they earn so little per hour that I can't ask them to go way up there and take those chains down." I assured him that I would be over to take care of it, then laughed to myself because I did the job yearly without getting paid anything for it.

Even audience members did not always feel secure during early Christmas Concerts on campus. "Staying awake was no problem" for A. Bruce Jacobs '77, whose first memory of the concert was a fear of falling to his death if he should happen to slip through the slats of the gray, splintered bleachers brought in for the concert from the football field.

It was Jim Cermak, really, who lifted the technical standards of the Christmas Concerts to a higher plane beginning in 1972. By affiliating the expertise and equipment of the theatre program with a more ambitious theoretical approach to the concerts, he brought significant benefits to both during his 22-year Christmas Concert tenure.

He also brought a new and valuable perspective to the concerts—one that would help nurture their growth. Cermak looked at the concerts as a theatrical, and therefore transitory, event: "It was an ephemeral thing that was happening. It wasn't supposed to be for all time, but for this specific season and for a particular group of people who have gathered together to commemorate it. For a little while, it exists on an ethereal plane, and then it goes away and we go on to something else."

That philosophy was shared by Paul Christiansen and Cy Running. Christiansen felt that the music, maybe especially the interludes, was not intended to last for all time as some monumental piece of sacred choral music. And Running termed the mural "poster art," meaning that it was intended to be viewed *for the moment*, like a quick snapshot in time. "You put it up, and then you take it down and put it away," Cermak affirmed.

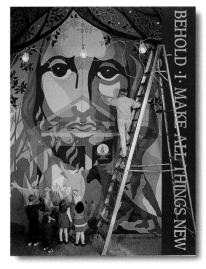

BEHOLD, I MAKE ALL THINGS NEW

Minneapolis concert preceded Moorhead concert thanks to a booking by Joan Sutherland at Orchestra Hall

Conductors:	René Clausen
	Christopher Cock
	J. Robert Hanson
Narrator:	Peter Halverson

For the first time, live models were used on the program cover in 1990. Bruce Hoium coached his daughter (seated) and others for the finished photo.

SENT FORTH BY GOD'S BLESSING

Christmas Concerts nationally televised to commemorate Concordia's centennial

Conductors: René Clausen
                Christopher Cock
                J. Robert Hanson

Narrators: Peter Halverson
                Solveig Haugland

MAKING IT WORK

Transforming a barn-like gymnasium into a concert hall was no mean challenge. But several methods were employed to do just that. Certainly placement of the mural and other artwork (then located on the north end of the Field House) was primary. Most of the athletic banners in the building were temporarily taken down, and the huge basketball scoreboard dangling from the central ceiling girders was lifted up and out of the audience's direct line of sight.

Then there were the trees—dozens of green spruce—some tall and slender, some short and squat, but all fragrant enough to mask the usual sweatsock odor of the Field House. It *smelled* like Christmas. Music manager Kurt Wycisk always arranged for the trees to be delivered, and workers from Concordia's physical plant first sprayed them with a fire retardant, then artfully arranged them in wooden bleacher sections adjacent to either side of the choir risers.

Jim Cermak recalled walking into the Field House one evening for a rehearsal and striding past the "forest," as it was affectionately known. "I did a double-take—there was a deer head sticking out from between the trees. It was Kurt's way of lightening the load—because we spent several intense weeks of our lives there," he laughed.

Working 72 hours straight was not uncommon for Cermak and his technical crew of students. "I was sleeping on the high-jump mats under a pile of coats and scared the living daylights out of a janitor," Cermak remembered. "Crews came in five shifts—first painters, then physical plant employees, then my lighting

crew after everyone else had left. Then Kurt would come in with his house managers and Field House employees to set up chairs, and finally the orchestra or brass ensemble would come in to rehearse. Scheduling all that was Kurt's responsibility, and he slowly started handing it off to me, piece by piece."

Technical director Jim Cermak supervised Christmas Concert production in Moorhead and Minneapolis for 22 years.

As many as 30 student volunteers would work nearly 1,000 hours on lighting during that period, some individu-ally putting in up to 40 hours over a five-day span. Nearly every piece of equipment on campus was commandeered for use during the Christmas Concerts. Lighting instruments and dimmer boards from the theatre and Student Productions were assembled into a unified system, safely hung, focused and gelled high over the heads of the audience.

As a student, Bryan Duncan '90 remembered the demanding process: "I was pulling up 30-pound lighting instruments on a rope from the top of the scaffolding. Starting at ten o'clock at night until five or six o'clock in the morning, we'd be lifting them, arm-over-arm, and we could hardly move the next day."

But the discomfort wasn't yet over. After nearly every concert, adjustments needed to be made. Workers often had to literally climb from scaffolds like monkeys

O COME, ONE AND ALL

Conductors: René Clausen
Christopher Cock
J. Robert Hanson
Narrators: Peter Halverson
Maura Cock

Tone and mood were created partly through effective lighting.

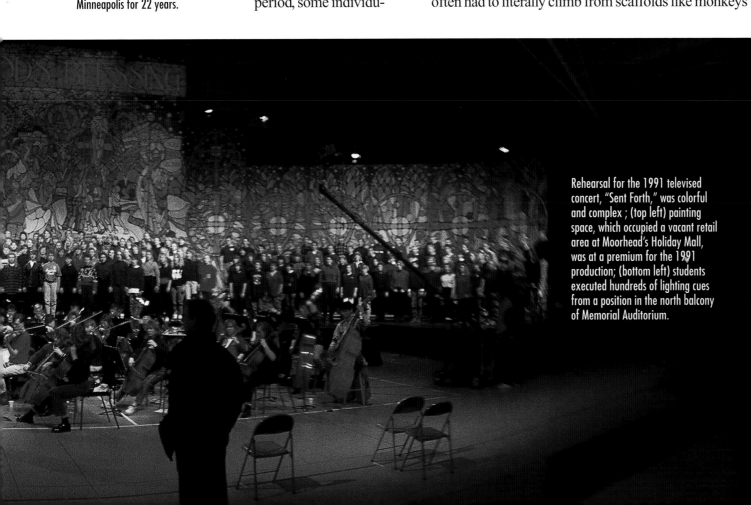

Rehearsal for the 1991 televised concert, "Sent Forth," was colorful and complex ; (top left) painting space, which occupied a vacant retail area at Moorhead's Holiday Mall, was at a premium for the 1991 production; (bottom left) students executed hundreds of lighting cues from a position in the north balcony of Memorial Auditorium.

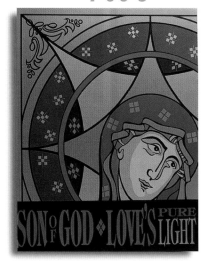

SON OF GOD, LOVE'S PURE LIGHT

Conductors:	René Clausen
	Christopher Cock
	June Boyd
	J. Robert Hanson
Narrators:	Peter Halverson
	Maura Cock

up to the pipes supported by basketball backboard standards. Hanging precariously, they checked loose cable connections, replaced lamps and refocused instruments. A new trussing system and hydraulic lifts eventually eased both the difficulty of the process and its associated trauma. Then the emphasis could more easily turn from the concert's mechanics to its aesthetics.

'CHRISTMAS FIREWORKS'

There was a time when Paul Christiansen expressed some concern that the Christmas Concerts might be evolving into more than a concert. He and Cermak discussed the impact of the art and whether the lighting effort might be getting too theatrical. "I understood that he didn't want the various elements to be competing with each other," Cermak asserted, "but whether you call it a 'concert' or a 'performance,' it's a theatrical event. When you have people in costumes (choir robes) marching around you with a brass ensemble (in the days before the orchestra) and you have 5,000 people in the audience standing, sitting, singing and reading—that was a theatrical event, only like some huge church service." Their chat ended amicably, and the lighting continued to support and enhance, rather than compete for the audience's attention.

Power requirements for the concerts gradually increased, necessitating both imagination and courage on the part of the technical staff. This was a gymnasium, after all, and its electrical service was something less than dynamic. Care had to be taken not to overload delicate circuits; rotary fans were used to cool dimmer packs manually. Always, there were more lighting instruments than receptacles, so cables were constantly being replugged to assure electrical integrity and eliminate (or, at least, reduce) the possibility of electrical failure. Normally, this procedure worked well—but not always, according to Cermak. During the Saturday

evening Christmas Concert in 1985, everything was going as scheduled when, without warning, the auditorium went *pitch black!*

"Son of God, Love's Pure Light" incorporated an iconographic-style mural in 1993.

I was calling the lighting cues from the back (south end) of the Field House when all of the circuit breakers went out simultaneously. Luckily, the singers knew what they were doing. In total darkness, they finished one piece and a single voice—the soloist for the next song—came up, singing clearly.

In the meantime, I sprinted down the hallway and into the power room. The breakers were hot, so I used my handkerchief and my tie as hotpads to protect my hands, and I reset the breakers and held them open until they cooled off enough. As I ran past the booth in the north balcony, I had yelled up to my crew and told them, "Bring everything to zero!"

Once the breakers were open again, we gradually brought the lights back up. The audience thought it was a marvelous effect.

Occasionally, other lighting challenges were presented by the artwork itself. Our conscious attempts to make each mural look different sometimes yielded surprising results. One year, for example, I decided to do the entire project using a reflective, metallic paint. With two shades of gold, a silver and a copper, plus black and white, we achieved quite a regal look, I thought. But two problems emerged. First, we were using oil-based paint instead of the usual latex and, as it turned out, every color required a *different* solvent to clean the brushes. Choosing the wrong solvent immediately turned the leftover paint on one's brush into a sticky, gummy glob—and my painters threatened to turn me into one of those globs, too. Our second complication was that the angle of the light bouncing off that highly reflective surface looked quite different, depending upon where audience members were seated. This I discovered when I overheard someone disappointedly remark, "They used to do it in color."

Christmas Concert photographs from the mid '60s show Field House lighting fixtures numbering approximately one dozen hanging from a suspended pipe. By the early '80s, that number had nearly quadrupled, and when Jim Cermak resigned from his Christmas Concert duties to devote more time to his teaching and theatre

As recently as 1972, only one dozen lighting instruments were enlisted to illuminate both choirs and mural.

responsibilities, the number had grown to nearly one hundred. "The excitement of my life," Cermak reflected, "has been working with the people who have helped make this concert happen. It's like Christmas fireworks. For a little while, we all sit back and sigh, 'O-o-o-o-o-h!' and 'A-a-a-a-a-h!' and feel down deep within us something wonderful. Then we are allowed to go on to the other things in our lives, to do what needs to be done."

As the torch was passed in 1995 from Cermak to former student Bryan Duncan— by then the full-time campus lighting director—the tradition of lighting excellence continued and expanded. Periodic television broadcasts of the concerts required even more lighting than normal. For the 1997 concert, it took 4,200 amps to power 300 instruments. "If anything had gone wrong," Duncan joked, "we might have browned-out most of south Moorhead."

David Hetland and Jim Cermak explored and expanded the visual possibilities of the Christmas Concerts.

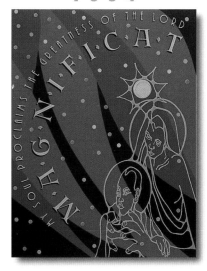

MAGNIFICAT

Daniel Moe served as interim conductor while René Clausen was on sabbatical leave

Conductors:	Daniel Moe
	Christopher Cock
	June Boyd
	J. Robert Hanson
Narrators:	Peter Halverson
	Maura Cock

Airborne particles of water vapor from a "fog machine" have helped add dramatic effect to the lighting.

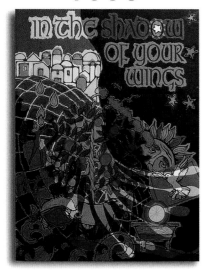

IN THE SHADOW OF YOUR WINGS

Conductors: René Clausen
                    Paul Nesheim
                    Bruce Houglum
                    June Rauschnabel
Narrators: Peter Halverson
                    Kathy Valan

Bryan Duncan, Bruce Jacobs and Tim Tommerson discussed technical issues prior to the 1997 television production.

His sophisticated, computerized lighting system allowed Bryan to add a "whole other dimension to reinforce more strongly" the message of the concerts. "Let Heaven and Nature Sing," the 1997 concert, was the inaugural event for the new computer board:

We actually were running two different light boards for the concert: one running conventional lights, one tracking moving lights. We were able to illustrate the Creation of the earth—it started out in blackness, then went to blue, and then the sun came out and moved up to the mural. And as that happened, the audience saw the lights come up as the sun rose. It was just a wonderful experience.

Every year, Bryan and I carefully study and discuss mural images and color possibilities. And despite his excitement about new technology, Bryan is conscientious about simply "trying to help tell the story."

"If the Christmas Concerts become a show about lighting, then we've failed," he said.

ENHANCING THE SOUND

Technological audio innovations since the Christiansen years have been subtle but steady, especially at the Moorhead concerts. Few audience members are ever aware of any electronic wizardry at work as they listen to the crystal-clear tones of choirs and orchestra and hear the "voice of God" boldly booming overhead.

It began with a single microphone and an old public-address system through which the narrator could be heard—at least in some parts of the auditorium. None of the music could be effectively amplified, so it fell to strong voices and the natural building resonance to carry the sound to the audience, who occasionally strained to hear the subtleties.

Philip Thompson recounted one of Cy Running's

early facetious contributions to the effort:

During a Christmas Concert rehearsal in the Field House, Paul J. wanted a soloist to sing from

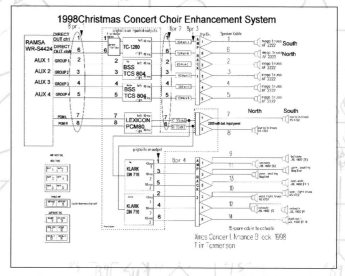

Computer-generated schematic drawings were produced to detail the complex audio setup. (Background: detail of television lighting schematic)

one of the side rooms to create the sound of a distant voice. To achieve the effect, he carefully set the door slightly ajar. While the soloist was in the room singing, Cy quietly crept over to the door, took out a tape measure and carefully read the distance between the door edge and the jamb. After pondering the measurement briefly, he walked away nodding as if to say, "Yes, that is precisely the correct distance."

Eventually, it fell to Bruce Jacobs, an acoustical specialist, to develop a system of "audio enhancement" for the Christmas Concerts in 1991. At the time, Jacobs was head of engineering at Prairie Public Television in Fargo, North Dakota, and he approached the college about the possibility of producing a one-hour show to air that same year. Because it was Concordia's centennial year, his concept was quickly approved, and plans were developed to accommodate this project.

Everything from art and illumination to acoustics had to be bigger and better than ever before. That year's mural increased in size threefold. Lighting more than doubled its intensity. And René Clausen was "rightfully concerned" about the potential for sound deterioration, according to Jacobs.

Working with Tim Tommerson '73, then a Concordia sound technician, Jacobs added a dozen microphones and nearly two dozen suspended speakers to accomplish the task. Calling it the "most challenging psychoacoustic project (audio system) I have ever designed," Jacobs conceded that it was also tricky to operate. Ultimately, the objective of making a very large room sound small and intimate was reached. Incorporating 18 speakers with 14 amplifier channels, Jacobs would eventually dub this his "proudest achievement."

Tommerson, who for many years supervised the enhancement system, explained that it had two key aims: to make the choirs seem "closer" to the audience at the back of the auditorium and to add reverberation to make the space seem "alive," even though it is jammed to capacity with people.

Each year, audio recordings under the supervision of Kerry Horst '88 are made for distribution to radio stations throughout the country. One of the complications in trying to tape during actual concerts is the constant coughing of audience members. It seems almost a grand conspiracy—that all that hacking, sneezing and nose-blowing must occur during the most quiet, intimate portions of the program. As if scripted, everyone lets loose like a huge flock of honking geese. Cy Running often threatened to glue a cough drop to each program.

Page turns throughout the concert are carefully planned to occur at optimum points—between selections or before audience hymns. Even the paper stock for the printed programs is selected to minimize their noise potential. Still, this act often reinforces the coughing, sounding like an immense flutter of wings from that same unruly flock of geese.

Distractions of *any* kind can often become an annoyance. Karl Christiansen '53, son of Concordia's legendary football coach Jake Christiansen, remembered just such an incident involving his younger sister:

Sonja '57 was repeatedly annoyed by a couple of young boys occupying the seats next to hers. She can be a "no-nonsense" sort of woman at times. She handled this situation by reaching across the first boy and grabbing the second boy by the shirt. She pulled their heads together and whispered, "If you two make another sound, I'm going to beat the (expletive deleted) out of you!" Problem resolved.

Tim Tommerson helped develop the subtle, 14-channel acoustical enhancement for the concerts.

NOW THE SILENCE, NOW THE FEAST

Conductors: René Clausen
Paul Nesheim
Bruce Houglum
June Rauschnabel
Narrator: Peter Halverson

"King of Kings" was the first major Christmas Concert recording produced for sale on both 45-rpm platters and reel-to-reel tape.

Bruce Jacobs (right) designed and supervised the Field House audio systems, including the Christmas Concert enhancement.

LET HEAVEN
AND NATURE SING

Television broadcast

Conductors: René Clausen
Paul Nesheim
Bruce Houglum
June Rauschnabel
Narrator: Peter Halverson

Here viewed from the top of the mural, full rehearsals in Moorhead required both tolerance and discipline.

SET 'EM UP AND SHIP 'EM OUT

Since 1952, the use of Concordia's Field House for the concert has been a key to its growth and success. Though the facility is not without some logistical problems, every attempt has been made to create as little inconvenience for the physical education department as possible. Through the years, Field House managers, including Irv Christenson, Don Krause, Art Lysne, Bob Nick '65 and Armin Pipho, have worked diligently to accommodate the music department's Christmas Concert needs as they generously have shared their facility. Now, with the addition of the Olson Forum athletic facilities, some of the pressure on the Field House has been relieved. Even so, careful coordination and considerate cooperation remain important ingredients to the success of the Moorhead concerts.

During a design class one morning in 1966, Cy Running was talking with us about the Christmas Concert production. "For those of you who plan to become teachers," he admonished, "remember that if you really want to get something done, don't go to the principal or the administration—go see the custodian."

His was the voice of experience, having relied upon Concordia's physical plant staff to do everything from building and priming the mural panels to carefully erecting the art and risers for each year's concert. And always, these tasks were accomplished with good humor, pride and care. To this day, even though the project is vastly more ambitious and demanding, that tradition continues.

Seating in the Field House was at first available only on a general-admission basis and always jammed to the rafters. "Tickets" consisted of freewill offering envelopes and, according to Jim Cermak, the full houses and long lines were largely due to the genius of music manager Kurt Wycisk. "He would hand out six to eight thousand tickets for five thousand seats," Cermak said with a grin. "Memorial Auditorium would be filled to overflowing—marginally illegal,

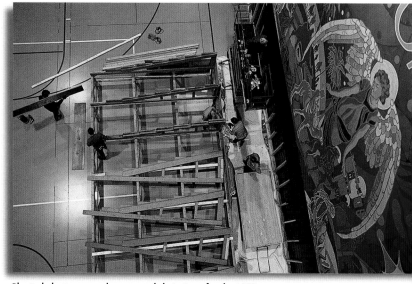

Physical plant personnel constructed choir risers for the 1992 concert.

fire-marshal capacity. Yet that cluster of people would come together, and their energy fed back into the music, the movement, into the people in the concert and the mural and the lights, and that's what made it electric."

Dale Lammi remembered people arriving by midafternoon to throw coats over rows of chairs, saving them for friends and relatives who would be coming later for the eight o'clock concert. "Of course, in more recent years," he joked, "if you ate fish dinner (*torsk*) or attended the President's Dinner first, then you got seated into a select, roped-off area in the permanent seating. But on the main floor and in the bleachers, people were still crammed in like sardines—your knees were in your teeth, almost, but nobody cared."

Finally, in 1985, reserved seating was eased into place—first in the permanent seating only and later, when the stage was moved to the west end of the auditorium, in the floor seats as well. This relieved the tedious early-bird stakeouts and the growing uncertainty of gate receipts. Today, all four Moorhead concerts are routinely sold out several weeks in advance.

Nearly since the concert's beginning, it has fallen to the college's physical plant, primarily the carpentry department, to assemble and dismantle the Moorhead concert. With the mural carefully erected and reinforced to the back wall of the Field House, assembly begins on the risers and side stages. This is precise work—no wood slivers or half-sunk screws are allowed. And, in fact, there never are any.

Kurt Wycisk's marketing "genius" brought expanded growth and demand to the Christmas Concerts.

Following the final concert in the Field House, everything is removed and the mural is carefully loaded for the trip down to Orchestra Hall.

Adding the Orchestra Hall venue in 1974 created an immediate need for technical improvisation. Because the Hall was built strictly as a concert house, lighting equipment was limited, and creative options were few. There the instruments were clamped to metal pipe "trees" located in each of the three balconies on either side of the stage. Although recent upgrades in equipment and instrument location have helped to expand lighting opportunities, no front lighting was possible in the early days.

Furthermore, the stage was not wide enough to display the mural fully without slanting the first and last panels at a 45-degree angle. As choirs have annually increased their membership, and with the addition of the orchestra, the space at Orchestra Hall has become extremely tight. Even with plywood stage extensions reaching over the first three rows of seating, it remains cramped. Choir members had to improvise on-stage seating arrangements, said Laura Moenke '98: "You didn't want to be in the front row. When the choir was seated, you'd have to sit on the floor or perched on other people's knees and feet."

Conductors and technicians continue to discuss plans to deal with these limitations by controlling future ensemble growth.

Concordia's motor pool must also be prepared for the Minneapolis sojourn. Today, relatively few college vans are used for this event because nearly all of the students travel on chartered buses. But in earlier days, according to Don and Helen (Oltman) '56 Krause, nearly 20 vans were employed to transport students and staff. "It was the time of year when you could have freezing rain or snow," said Don, "so it was always a worry that they would get down and back again safely."

"We prayed for three days," added Helen.

Amen.

SHOUT THE GLAD TIDINGS

Conductors: René Clausen
Paul Nesheim
Bruce Houglum
June Rauschnabel
Narrator: Peter Halverson

When only general-admission tickets were available in the '70s, audience members arrived hours early to assure a good seat.

1974 concert at Orchestra Hall

1993 concert, "Son of God, Love's Pure Light"

Chapter 6

SENT FORTH

Outreach

I was the only person in the newly built auditorium until a man in a khaki suit walked out on the stage, carrying a huge set of blueprints. I told him of the long run of concerts in Moorhead and how unbelievably great it would be to have the Christmas Concert at Orchestra Hall.

He was the building's architect, as it turned out. After giving me an extensive tour of "his" building, highlighting all the acoustical enhancements, he asked me, "What date did you say you wanted?" Sympathetic to my cause, the architect introduced me to Orchestra Hall manager Barry Hoffman. When I told Barry the desired date, December 20, a look of astonishment crossed his face.

*"Every other Friday of the entire year has been reserved," he said. "Only one Friday night is **not** reserved by the Orchestra: Friday, December 20!" The concert was a go!*

—John S. Pierce

Since their early years, the Christmas Concerts have been Concordia's "Christmas gift to the Midwest" – an annual event that touches thousands aesthetically and spiritually through word, music and art. Miss Duea and her college Music Club aimed "to promote an appreciation of 'better music' in the community," and that idea of outreach continues to this day.

Making the concerts a community event was only the beginning. Reaching a broader constituency through the Christmas Radio Parties was another step. As word of Concordia's unique Christmas experience spread, people began coming from greater distances to attend the event. Following the gas rationing of World War II, the concert expanded into three successive evenings in 1946, then four in 1949 and five in 1951. And by the mid '70s, at the height of Paul J. Christiansen's conducting career, additional performances of the concerts were brought to Orchestra Hall in Minneapolis.

Today, the Christmas Concerts continue to pack the concert halls in Moorhead and Minneapolis each year. Taped radio broadcasts take place through the Christmas season. And in this visual age, the concerts reach out to new audiences through the medium of tele-

Adapting the mural and risers to Orchestra Hall's diminutive stage took imagination and compromise.

vision. More subtly, this outreach has also been carried on by Concordia alumni who have openly copied the Christmas Concert formats in events at other high schools and colleges across the country—and even in other nations. Together, all these opportunities point to the potential for huge increases in listening and viewing audiences—people who will see and hear the message conveyed through mural and music.

Presidential Praise

Concordia College president Paul J. Dovre received an unexpected letter following the nationally televised Christmas Concert in 1991, the college's centennial year.

Former U.S. President Richard M. Nixon had viewed the concert at home with his wife, Pat.

For the Nixons, the Concordia Christmas Concert was "the finest T.V. event of the Christmas season."

RICHARD NIXON

WOODCLIFF LAKE, NEW JERSEY

12-17-91

Dear Mr. President,

Mrs. Nixon & I were privileged to hear the Concordia Christmas program last night & we want to express our appreciation to all of those who participated for producing what for us was the finest T.V. event of the Christmas season.

Enclosed is a modest token of our appreciation —

With best wishes for the New Year —

Sincerely,

Richard Nixon

Former President Richard Nixon responded to the 1991 television broadcast of the Concordia Christmas Concert with a letter and a check.

Anyone would jump at the chance to bring a small-college choir's performance to Orchestra Hall … right? Surprisingly, the decision to add Orchestra Hall as a Christmas Concert venue, even for the well-known Concordia Choir, was anything but automatic.

Beginning in the early '70s, a number of Concordia alumni became strong advocates for bringing the concerts to the Twin Cities of Minneapolis and St. Paul, 240 miles down Interstate Highway 94. John Pierce, who was assistant alumni director, pointed out that, in the first place, there were more Concordia alumni in the Minneapolis-St. Paul area than in Fargo-Moorhead, providing a natural audience of supporters. Second, St. Olaf College—the only other college in the area producing Christmas Concerts of the same magnitude and quality as Concordia's—held its concerts on its campus in Northfield, south of the Cities. So a Concordia Christmas Concert in the Twin Cities proper would be the only one of its kind.

John Pierce laid the groundwork for expanding the Christmas Concerts into the Twin Cities market.

"I thought the choir had already paid the price of preparation," said Pierce. "Why *not* pack up the backdrops, instruments and musicians and take them to the Twin Cities?"

Pierce and others, however, did meet with some resistance from both the administration and those involved in the concerts. After the extensive rehearsals and the intense concert experience, choir members had to prepare for final exams the following week. They wouldn't want to give up Christmas vacation, after finals, to give a concert in Minneapolis. And there was skepticism about transporting students and the large murals, and about whether the artwork would be as effective (it isn't, as it turns out) in a hall specifically designed for musical performances rather than theatre. Finally, of course, was the question of how the college would pay for such a venture. Transportation, food and lodging, and hall rental costs were sure to be expensive.

Turned down once in 1970, Pierce "went back to the well" every year until, in 1974, he was given the OK to test the waters in Minneapolis-St. Paul—with some very clear parameters. In order to promote the Christmas Concert in the Twin Cities, Pierce and his supporters would have to find:

- a facility acceptable to the choir
- a facility available on the single acceptable date: Friday, December 20
- $13,000 to cover expenses

"If the above requirements are met, you may suggest the idea to Paul J. Christiansen and the choir," Pierce was told. "They will vote on it. *Only* if they agree will it happen."

Pierce headed to the Twin Cities, where he met with Dr. Carl Granrud, head of Lutheran Brotherhood Insurance Company. Granrud and his associate, Gretchen Pracht, suggested three potential concert venues: Augsburg College's Melby Auditorium, the St. Paul Civic and O'Shaughnessy Auditorium at St. Catherine's University. However, none

Instrumental options were expanded in 1986 with the inclusion of the Concordia Orchestra.

In recent years, tickets to the Minneapolis Christmas Concerts were a rare commodity, as the concerts sold out quickly.

Detail from the 1995 mural

was available on Friday, December 20. And Pierce only managed to raise $2,000 of the necessary funds—$1,000 of it from Lutheran Brotherhood. "After two days, I was ready to pack it in," he said.

Before Pierce headed home, though, Pracht suggested he look over the soon-to-be-completed Minnesota Orchestra Hall. It was a gorgeous, $15 million masterpiece designed to provide outstanding acoustics. Pracht warned Pierce that the Hall would be reserved by the Orchestra *every* Friday night; but perhaps he could make plans there for another year.

It was this visit that led to Pierce's encounter with the architect who introduced him to Barry Hoffman. Concordia had Orchestra Hall on Friday, December 20, if that was what was wanted. Paul J. and the choir voted yes. But there was still one hitch.

Pierce had to confess to choir manager Kurt Wycisk that he'd only raised a fraction of the money.

Music manager Kurt Wycisk and Concordia president Joseph Knutson helped establish the long relationship with Daggett Trucking of Frazee, Minnesota.

At that time, there was no charge for tickets to the Moorhead concerts. "Don't worry," Kurt told Pierce. "If we charge four or five dollars a ticket in the Cities, that will be enough, with the $2,000 you've raised, to cover expenses."

Paul Dovre, academic dean at the time, was asked whether it would be acceptable for students to miss additional class time for the Minneapolis experience: "That was kind of a dunk shot, but I went out on a limb and said, 'Of course.' It made sense to do it."

Members of the Twin Cities branch of the Concordia Alumni Association—Herb Morgenthaler '61, Marshall Johnson '58, Don Bihrle

Paul Christiansen and Marshall Johnson entertained student musicians at a dinner event sponsored by Twin Cities alumni.

'60, Gerry Bjelde '56 and Mark Halaas met with Wycisk in Minneapolis to discuss the first Minneapolis Christmas Concert and how to market it. Ticket prices were set at $3 for adults and $2 for students. Invitations were sent to Concordia alumni, parents and friends within a 100-mile radius of Minneapolis-St. Paul. Halaas wrote copy for the mailer, and it worked: by return mail, the college managed to sell out one whole concert and half of a second.

Since Orchestra Hall was available the previous

night as well, the Twin Cities concerts were held on Thursday and Friday to accommodate the enthusiastic response. For the following year's trip, the choir decided to schedule two concerts on the same night, in part to allow more study time for finals after the concerts were over. After a quarter-century of performances, that doubleheader is now as much a tradition in the Twin Cities as the Christmas Concerts are in Moorhead.

NEW BUILDING, NEW RULES

Physically getting everyone—singers, conductors, orchestra players and their instruments, narrators, a few painters and production people—down to Orchestra Hall is a logistical feat in itself, coordinated each year by the choir manager.

Transporting the murals is a huge undertaking.

Moorhead Christmas Concert admission went from a freewill offering system to reserved-seating tickets.

Ticket Trivia

Tickets have often been a nightmare for choir managers and ticket sellers, who scramble to fill requests from literally thousands of hopeful concert goers. Still,

Reserved seat tickets to the four Moorhead concerts are sold in the foyer of Concordia's Outreach Center.

the system is much improved over the previous lack of one.

J.L. Rendahl, long-time choir manager, public relations director and admissions vice president for the college, once told the story of a concert at the Moorhead Armory: "Quite an extensive advertising campaign was conducted, and it was a beautiful evening, and the Armory was full and 1,000 people were standing outside. It was necessary for me to mount the truck and explain to the 1,000 people standing outside why they couldn't come in. Beginning with the next year, we put out a certain number of tickets. That plan's been used ever since."

Choir managers are always aware of the demand for tickets. Wayne Wagstrom began receiving requests in mid-October for the 1950 concert, opening as many as 90 request letters in a single mail delivery.

Until 1985, freewill offering envelopes were used as tickets for the Christmas Concerts. Donald Krause noted that the "average donation was about 28 cents per person in the '50s." But they always afforded a few surprises when opened, reported Concordia's *Alumni News* in 1972.

In fact, some people went to great lengths to disguise the fact that their contributions were not legal tender, the publication noted: "In addition to about $9,200 to pay the bills, a varied assortment of items was contributed by concert attendees—things such as newspapers clipped to the size of paper money, play money, match folders, bus tokens and buttons."

Business manager Curt Danielson was quoted as saying the college had received Confederate money and flattened cigarette butts—and a lot of Bible verses.

'Smorgy' Promotes Christmas Concerts

Concordia got some unique press in 1950, when choir manager Wayne Wagstrom teamed up with *Minneapolis Morning Tribune* cartoonist Kurt Carlson. Wagstrom sent Carlson information about the concerts, along with photos of key personalities, who would then appear in the comic strip featuring the whimsical character, "Smorgy."

Every year on our way down to the Cities for the Orchestra Hall concert, we keep an eye out for a big green semi from Daggett Truck Line in Frazee, Minnesota. "The Daggett trucks were immediately there," remembered Jim Cermak. Music manager Gordon Moe said the college's positive relationship with the owner of the firm gave the project a boost:

I think that Kurt Wycisk, as resourceful as he was, gave Marvin Daggett a call to say, "The only way this is going to happen is if I can get someone to transport our equipment." And ever since then, Daggett has loaned the use of their finest semi-tractor and trailer and their best drivers. I can remember my first year on the job, timidly calling Daggett to ask about transportation. I talked with a gentleman named LaVerne "Max" Maxwell and he quickly said, "Of course, we're going to do this."

When the panels were unloaded into Orchestra Hall the first time, Cermak and his crew were met with a list of rules, designed to protect the sparkling new building. "No scratches on the floors or walls" was number one. Cermak remembered:

The first thing that happened was that the flats were too wide to get them in the double doorways—because Orchestra Hall is not used to moving scenery in. We had to bend the flats. We had to literally curve—make them bow—so that they would fit through the doorways. We would slide them along the floor on the brand new carpeting, leaving little flecks of paint, little colored marks along the walls where it scraped. At one point, the stagehands took off an exit sign—they were going down the hallway at breakneck speed with this flat, thinking that they had cleared all the obstacles, and all of a

Music manager Gordon Moe (center) directed the loading process as mural panels were transported from a Fargo shopping mall where they were painted to the Field House.

sudden they heard this massive "C-A-A-R-A-C-K!" And there went an exit sign, just hanging out in the middle of the hallway. It was as if we had broken the fingers of a small child.

For the next year's concert, Cermak built the mural frames out of redwood one-by-sixes, like theatre flats. "Everything was going really well until the theatre stage hands at Orchestra Hall said, 'Oh, we just stand them up this way. We do it in stage shows all the time. It's not a problem.' *C-A-A-R-A-C-K!* They split that thing in half. It just folded over on itself."

It was not the first time massive repairs had been made, nor would it be the last—although in recent years, our touch-up and repair needs seem mercifully to have lessened. In succeeding years, the panels were built of reinforced two-by-fours for greater strength. One year, however, a smaller panel was actually left behind in Moorhead, and a U-Haul had to be hired to truck it down.

When the Minneapolis concerts began, the mural design had to be changed to accommodate the different structures in Orchestra Hall. One panel had to be left out entirely, so the artist had to take that into consideration. Paul Allen was mural designer at the time:

We put all the paint in huge garbage cans, and we sealed them up, taped them up—or we should have. I remember we were backing up to the dock there at Orchestra Hall, and one of them tipped over and some of the cans opened up and then we had paint in the van. I thought, "Oh, Don Krause (head of Concordia's motor pool) is going to love this."

Krause would later describe the same incident as "adding several new colors to the floor carpet and inside walls of the van."

At Orchestra Hall, the meticulous Allen was once again hurried in his touch-ups to the mural, this time because of security rules.

Don Krause provided college vans to students and staff for early Minneapolis concert trips.

In 1977, its fourth year in Minneapolis, Orchestra Hall continued to provide audiences with a beautiful setting and superior acoustics.

Paul laughed as he remembered:

They had a timer on the doors, and we absolutely had to be out of there at a certain time, or that was it—you know, we'd have to stay overnight there or something. At least, I remember I was scared about it. I thought, "We really gotta get outta here, or the fire department's gonna come or some horrendous thing." So we did. We were outta there, but it was down to about three minutes—it was "mission impossible."

1980 mural on the stage at Orchestra Hall

Detail from the 1995 mural

Over the years, I've often said the Christmas Concert *looks* better in Moorhead, and *sounds* better in Minneapolis. For choir and orchestra, the Minneapolis concerts sound glorious—although, as the numbers in the choirs have swelled, I get claustrophobic just looking at them packed onto the risers and jammed, with the orchestra, onto the stage. But for singers, it's a powerful experience. "Latecomers poured down the aisles as the choirs sang 'O Come, All Ye Faithful,'" said Ann (Schroeder) Taylor '93. "It was so moving to see streams of people coming to our call to worship!"

For technical directors, the "look" of the concerts at Orchestra Hall presents unique challenges. Designed almost strictly for orchestral performances, "Orchestra Hall is definitely not a place to do lighting," said Bryan Duncan. In 1974, the hall had perhaps one-tenth the equipment it has today, and the concert had to be lighted only from the side balconies. No front light was available, yet Cermak had to light not only the mural, but the entire choir and brass ensemble.

When Cermak was on leave in 1981, lights "popped" on and off during the Minneapolis concert—

it made me cringe. In the darkness of Orchestra Hall, a hand came out from the row behind me and patted my shoulder. It was the kindest thing that could have happened to me—I turned around and saw that it was Eleanor Christiansen, and I thought, "It's going to be OK."

"Whatever years it's been, the lighting at Concordia is going to be better than the lighting in Minneapolis," said Duncan. "There's no way around it. You definitely get your sound quality there, but … they have a few lighting trees on the sides, and that's what you get to do all of your lighting with."

In fact, Bryan has found only two opportunities when he can really do something with lighting the mural at Orchestra Hall: "We like the beginning of the concert when there's no light on stage, and we like the end of the concert when there's nobody in front of the mural, and the lights are down in the front. Those are the two mo-

Bryan Duncan expanded both the scale and the technology of Christmas Concert lighting after he became technical director.

ments we get when we're in Minneapolis, whereas in Moorhead we have moments all over the place."

Theatre student Evelyn (Panula) Weston '82 ran the backstage lighting board at Orchestra Hall.

Wearing a headset and carrying a tiny flashlight to see his cues, Cermak, in the early days, would "call" the show for the lighting technicians from a seat in front of the stage. One year, someone was given Cermak's seat before the concert began:

I immediately went to Kurt (Wycisk) and said, "I can't start the show. There's somebody in my chair." Kurt had two tickets in the center section, where the college president and all the dignitaries usually sat. I took those two tickets, I walked down to where this woman was sitting in my seat, and I said, "For you and your companion,

Jim Cermak's substantial theatrical stage management experience paid big dividends when the concerts added the Orchestra Hall venue.

I have two tickets—it's about eight rows further back, but it's in the center of the auditorium. I need to sit here to call the show." And she said, "Absolutely not. I paid for these seats. I want these seats. I'm not moving." So I called the house manager and said, "I need a folding chair," and I set it up next to her. I sat next to her in the aisle, and I called the entire show there. She was very unhappy and did not enjoy the concert at all—and she told me about it every time there was a pause.

In retrospect, Cermak admitted, it was "not very funny"—nor were things always smooth even after a technical console was installed at the back of the auditorium:

I was coming from backstage, and we didn't have badges or passes. I would just walk on. The doors were locked. I said, "I need to get in," and they said, "I'm sorry, the concert is starting. We've been signaled to start, and we locked the doors."
"But you don't understand, I'm the technical director."
"Then you should have been in the auditorium already."
"But I'm not, you know."
I was very tired and aggravated, so I just sat down on the floor next to the auditorium. Inside, everybody was wondering what was going on. The choirs had already taken their places and everything, but I couldn't get in to my headset. All the ushers and house managers were running around saying, "How come it's not starting?" And someone said, "The technical director must be locked out." And so this house manager finally walked past me the second time and said, "Who are you?"
"I'm the technical director."
"We're supposed to start this concert."
"They won't let me in."

*"Well ... well, **I'll** let you in!"*
I walked in, sat down on the stool, put on the
headset and said, "Go!" for the first cue!

Making the trip to Minneapolis the week after the Moorhead concert is "easier than one might imagine," said Gordon Moe: "All the students are focused on doing an excellent job and presenting an excellent concert. They know we're going to down to present the best Christmas Concert we can and that we have a higher purpose. I think they respond to that very well." His biggest hitch? "One year the conductors thought I had arranged for a harpist to meet us at Orchestra Hall, and I thought *they* had arranged for the harpist. We ended up having to rent an electronic instrument down there."

One unpredictable factor has always been

Hauling students and instruments to Orchestra Hall each year is no small feat.

Herb Morgenthaler helped organize the Minneapolis Christmas Concerts.

Minnesota's winter weather—would snowstorms prevent the choir from making the trip? "I've always worried about that, year after year," said Herb Morgenthaler. "We have been so lucky. God was on our side." So far, the choir has been snowed in once, *in* Minneapolis—but never snowed *out* of it. Concordia's VISA card took a heavy hit for extra room and board that time.

That second run of concerts at Orchestra Hall

Reflecting on the Themes

Longtime Concordia president Paul Dovre, who retired in 1999, often addressed preconcert President's Dinner audiences on the thematic messages he saw and heard. Following are excerpts from some of those presentations:

Paul Dovre presided over his final President's Dinner in 1998 before retiring the following summer.

1995: *The concert ("In the Shadow of Your Wings") begins with the Creation story. The setting is rather dark and intimate and features an opening choral collage which frames the telling of the story. You have heard this story before, but I dare say you have never heard it told as you will hear and see and experience it tonight.*

1996: *Think of the silences of your year past . . . and contemplate the feast. Judged against this mood (the fast pace of our daily lives) the theme for our annual Concordia Christmas Concert ("Now the Silence, Now the Feast") stands and looks and sounds in sharp contrast.*

1998: *This year's theme is "Shout the Glad Tidings" and the mood is, unabashedly, celebrative. In the development of the theme the artists deal with the fundamental issues of time and eternity and in each case the ending is triumphant —even in the face of death itself.*

would not have happened without the support and foresight of the small group of alumni who sparked the first event, many of whom have continued to actively promote the Twin Cities performances. And it couldn't continue without the exceptional support we've received from the Orchestra Hall staff.

"I think we do have a special relationship with Orchestra Hall," said Moe. "The students have always treated the facility nicely. We have that history. We've been a successful event for Orchestra Hall, which they value, but they have also told me that they honor the relationship we have developed."

LUTEFISK AND LEFSE

Adding the concert venue at Orchestra Hall led to a number of other outreach efforts tying in with the Minneapolis performances. Annual President's Dinners have been hosted in Minneapolis since 1975, the second year the concert was given at Orchestra Hall. Originally alumni-only events, the dinners are now open to the public as well and are held in Minneapolis and Moorhead.

Paul Dovre was in his first year as Concordia's president when he hosted the first dinner in Minneapolis, introducing "in quite a modest way" the program that the audience would experience, with remarks based on notes and reflections from his attendance at the Moorhead concert. Later, Dovre's speeches included more extensive commentary about the music and art—a combination of information he gleaned from René and me and his own thoughtful message, putting the concert into the context of world events and the life around us.

It was five or six years before Moorhead began to host a President's Dinner on the Friday evening of the concerts—but concert goers never had to starve before that. Even in the 1920s and '30s, the college had hosted Christmastime Norwegian dinners for its mostly Scandinavian students and faculty. In 1960, a preconcert *smörgåsbord* get-together was initiated for alumni and friends, who were served by waitresses in traditional Norwegian costume. Receptions were also held for alumni and guests in Minneapolis, often at the downtown Athletic Club or at the YWCA across the street from Orchestra Hall. One of the first of these events was held at Orchestra Hall itself. "We weren't supposed to get the new carpet dirty," recalled Mark Halaas, "but for some unknown reason, the caterer prepared seasonal

With the Eagerness of a Child

Campus pastor Carl Lee always used the theme and experience of the Christmas Concert to reinforce his Advent message to students. "At that time of year, they need the warmth of the Gospel," Lee said. "For us, Advent extended from Thanksgiving to the first concert. After that, it was Christmas."

In the soft voice, almost a whisper, that was his trademark, Lee offered this prayer for Concordia Chapel during a Christmas Concert week:

Lord, Christmas is on my mind again.
I wait with the eagerness of a child for its coming.
I like to expect. I like to get ready.
I like the way the Christmas Concert helps me get focused.
I like to hear in word and song the extraordinary way God is saying that
the child Jesus is very near and I am very dear.

Lord, Christmas is on my mind as I await the Christmas Concert tonight.
Startle my routine. Stop my busyness.
Quiet my anxieties. Crank up my excitement.
Help me to get ready for finals.
Help me to get ready for Christmas.
Help me to be more open to your coming.
Tell me again tonight in the concert how special and loved I am.
Tell me again tonight the glad tidings of joy and the message of peace and
good will for all the world.
Come, O Come, Emmanuel.
Come, O Come, Prince of Peace. Amen.

cookies covered with powdered sugar. By the time we were done, it looked like it had snowed."

For a number of years, the Minneapolis Christmas Concerts also extended to Friday mornings, with a free concert for students from Minneapolis public and private schools. It was a different audience—"the kids always wanted to clap," observed Herb Morgenthaler. Those concerts were eventually discontinued.

In Moorhead, "A Children's Christmas" was observed in the mid '70s, when children's choirs from area congregations were invited to Concordia to put on a Christmas miniconcert of their own. Held in Concordia's chapel, the service soon came to be called "The Other Christmas Concert."

"That Sunday morning worship service during Christmas Concert weekend gave students and parents yet another opportunity to worship through the eyes of a child," said campus pastor Carl Lee.

IN THE TELEVISION AGE

Television has had a profound impact on our ability to bring the Christmas Concerts to an even wider and more visually astute audience. Early broadcasts of the concerts began in the '50s, as reported by the local *Red River Scene* in 1954:

In the misty December night, the streetlights glittered as giant stars and from the hulking shadow of a building, the Holy music of Christmas wrapped the air with the inspiration of the

Fargo's Prairie Public Television produced outstanding Christmas Concert broadcasts in 1988, 1991 and 1997.

Television cameras recorded two dress rehearsals and one live concert to obtain enough footage to edit the final one-hour presentation.

soul. It was one of the three nights. The musical strains resounding through the stone walls came from the nationally-famous Concordia College Choir, giving forth with its annual Christmas concert.

More than 11,000 citizens of the Red River Valley attended the three performances . . . . For the thousands of area residents who were unable to attend the Concordia Christmas concert this year, an opportunity to view portions of the production will be available when WDAY-TV presents a 15-minute film on December 23.

Shot by ELC Films of Minneapolis, the piece was also picked up by other area TV stations and broadcast on Christmas Eve by WCCO-TV in Minneapolis. Another half-hour program was presented by WDAY-TV of Fargo in 1963.

In 1980, stations throughout Minnesota, North Dakota and Montana also carried a 30-minute program produced by Lutherans of the Prairie. It included the college's famed choir and Christmas mural, as well as local and regional scenes. Christmas Concerts were televised in 1985, 1988, 1991 and 1997. In 1991, the college's centennial year, the massive concert with its huge mural was aired by nearly 200 stations in 55 states and territories.

Mounting a major television production is a daunting task for everyone involved. Potentially providing a national platform for airing the Christmas Concerts to millions of viewers, TV broadcasts entail a great deal of early planning and cooperation among musical, artistic and production participants. How will the presence of cameras affect audience and performers? How might it affect ticket sales and setup schedules? Will we really be able to pull this off? "I feel the concert is worthy of national exposure," said Gordon Moe. "But it's such a huge event, and to try to capture it on television is a massive task."

In 1997 we painted for two months solid on a mural that was three times its usual size to accommodate television production. It was worth the effort—but could not be done every year except on a smaller scale. Funding is also a factor. 1997's broadcast cost more than $100,000 to produce and air.

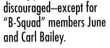

Public displays of affection among painters are discouraged—except for "B-Squad" members June and Carl Bailey.

Dwarfed by the central panels of the 1996 mural, "Now the Silence, Now the Feast," David Hetland completed his painting touchup.

Soul Food

Helen Stensrud, mother of painting assistant Karen Stensrud, has provided sandbakkel cookies for our final days of mural work in the Field House. It's now a tradition—one she is not allowed to forget—and in 1996, she sent this poem with the carefully packed cookies:

Sandbakkels are the soul food of
Concordia Christmas Concert
mural painters—
with flour, the base, like the background,
a necessary foil for striking line
and design,
butter for richness,
like the deep rich colors,
sugar for sweetness,
like symbols that tell the Christ-story,
egg, two yolks and a white,
to hold it all together,
like the artist's design
which expresses the theme,
and flavoring of almond or vanilla,
like accent colors, shading and surprises,
worked together smoothly, molded
with care, and baked until golden,
like a mural painted by a good crew.

Sandbakkels are the soul food of
Concordia Christmas Concert
mural painters—
with love and admiration
for your good work and what it says
to all who see and experience it.

For many people (myself included) it's just not Christmas until the concert music has been heard and the lighted spectacle of robed choirs in front of the huge mural has been seen. Carl and June Bailey take in not just one, but *every* Moorhead performance, enjoying the subtle differences of each concert. There are those for whom the concerts are an Advent tradition for the whole family. Christmas Concert audiences comprise all ages, from tiny babies to elderly people. They take buses from nursing homes and churches, drive from homes many miles away and even fly in from around the country especially for the concerts.

"I have always felt the Christmas message and the glorious Christmas spirit down to the marrow of my bones," wrote Haakon Carlson. There are many who attend the concerts year after year and some who attend them *all* every year. Mary Galbreath of Oakes, North

Lasting Memories

When people leave the Christmas Concert, they take a concert program home with them. It's not only a nice remembrance of the event, but is a scriptural, musical and prayer resource to which they can return over and over again during the Christmas season.

In recent years, concert goers also have had the opportunity to purchase other mementos of the concerts and choir. It's a form of outreach, said music manager Gordon Moe, that lets people relive the experience through the holiday season and beyond. Sweatshirts, a collector's series of ornaments (which take their design from the current year's mural and theme) and Concordia Choir recordings are all offered, building on the Christmas Concert tradition— and bringing it home.

A wide range of Christmas Concert memorabilia, including limited edition, laser-etched tree ornaments, embroidered shirts (modeled by "B-Squad" member June Bailey), compact discs and videos, has expanded the concerts' scope and impact.

Dakota, has introduced family and friends to this "gift of performance," adding, "It begins our Advent season." Concert goers Ron and Linda Anderson echoed

A long train ride brought some 50 high school students from Broadus, Montana, to the 1969 Concordia Christmas Concert.

the stories of many with their first trip to the Christmas Concert in the late '60s: "It was 130 miles back to Milbank, South Dakota. The temperature was minus 30 degrees as we began our trip home after an evening performance, and the heater in our car quit working. It was a cold, two-hour drive, but our spirits were warm from the beautiful music we had heard."

Julie Lindemann Slag first saw a Christmas Concert when her junior high music class made the trip in 1963. Harboring a secret love for singing, which "expressed some of my most deeply held spiritual feelings," the girl was overwhelmed by the crowds, elegant programs and the instrumentalists tuning. She had never heard an orchestra before:

We whispered to each other, crowded together on the hard wooden bleachers. Almost stifled in my heavy overcoat, I found myself holding my breath in anticipation, and then it was dark.

Christmas in Samoa

C. Robert Lewis '68 may hold the record for carrying the Christmas Concert tradition the farthest distance from Moorhead, Minnesota. Lewis spent 20 years in American Samoa, where he taught piano and music courses at American Samoa Community College and started a choir; his wife, Rosemary, began an instrumental music program.

"Samoans are tremendous musicians who have been singing and dancing for hundreds of years," wrote Bob Lewis, adding, "A Samoan can sing about 200 hymns from memory, despite having little knowledge of musical notation."

Lewis initiated the college's Concordia-style Christmas concerts in 1981, and they became extremely popular, running every year until the Lewises left the island in 1997—and drawing audiences and participants from all over Samoa. Since local high schools had no music programs, choir section leaders would visit the schools daily to teach Christmas music. Some years, the Christmas concert choir numbered 500 singers, harmonizing in the island's traditional, eight-part patterns. Concerts were given in English one night and Samoan the second, and taped by a local television station.

Lewis' concerts also featured a large mural backdrop, made of wood frames with masonite panels; cloth could not be used because of the humidity. Christmas trees were made of wood framing, chicken wire and palm fronds, and singers carried candles in coconut-shell bases.

"I remember one concert when the choirs recessed with their candles through the audience, singing Paul J. Christiansen's 'My Song in the Night,' " Lewis recounted. "That night was so calm with beautiful stars. Little did we know that 24 hours later, Hurricane Val would roar over our little island."

But the seed had been deeply planted, and the concerts are continuing.

Bob and Rosemary Lewis established multilingual, Concordia-style Christmas concerts in American Samoa that grew to include 500 singers and instrumentalists.

For many years, Casey Jones patterned his annual Festival Concert with The Colorado Choir after the Concordia production.

Chimes tolled behind the fir trees. Silence.

Trumpets sounded! Cymbals clashed! Lights appeared! From all parts of the Field House, columns of marching singers poured into the aisles singing. I found myself standing up—there was too much to see and too much to hear. I rubbed my face: tears!

My eyes were riveted to the central figure, the short, tuxedoed man. He seemed utterly focused, completely calm and controlled. And reverent. I remember thinking, "It's like he's offering up this music to God."

For students who participate in the Christmas Concerts, the influence is lasting. Jon R. Pederson '72 was leaving for Marine boot camp immediately following the performances in 1970. "You can imagine my emotions," he wrote. Meggan Manlove '98 was one of many singers who found that the discipline of rehearsals and the message of the concerts strengthened their faith: "In the midst of capstone courses and post-college planning I prayed through Dr. Clausen's setting of 'Psalm 150.' I was given words to thank God for the good in my life and the world."

It is almost impossible to measure the significance for these students, said Paul Dovre: "They're part of an event that takes incredible planning, that involves the highest levels of art that are possible at a collegiate level. I can't imagine anything like it." And the discipline of preparing and then, night after night, performing, can have "extraordinary" impact. For students like Janet Klemmer Hoberg '67, the concerts have inspired continued work in the arts:

I was an extremely homesick freshman until the Christmas Concert—the beauty of the artwork and the music helped me realize that I had chosen the right college for me. I have continued in art as a teacher and artist, and in music in several singing groups and as a soloist. I completed my Master of Arts degree in 1989. This would not have happened if I had quit in 1963.

Imitation is the sincerest form of flattery, and some of these alumni have gone on to found Concordia-esque Christmas concerts of their own in other states. In 34 years of directing choral music at Colorado State University, Edward Anderson presented a successful series of Christmas concerts, once conducting three concerts on a single Sunday to accommodate the season's listeners. His experiences at Concordia under his mentor, Paul J. Christiansen, were "obviously the catalyst for our presentations, as well as the pattern for his many alumni choral directors all over the land." People in Colorado were fortunate to get a large dose. Casey Jones conducted concerts at Adams State College in Alamosa, Colorado, between 1964 and 1984, drawing 6,000 people over a three-night run. Under Jones, Adams State and The Colorado Choir, based in Denver, also did combined concerts, which mirrored Concordia's in their use of choral music and art to reinforce a consistent theme. "Start and say something all the way through" was Jones' philosophy.

Paul J.'s son Sigurd '64 conducts annual Christ-

Ramona Forness replicated a smaller version of the 1984 Concordia Christmas Concert mural as a seasonal decoration for Calvary Lutheran Church in Grand Forks, N.D. She and several volunteers spent hundreds of hours painting the eight panels. "I finally had to walk away from it, because I was getting too picky," Ramona noted. During the terrible deluge of 1997, the entire church was flooded; the water stopped two inches below the mural's wooden framework.

mas concerts at Texas Lutheran University. Bruce Vantine '71 founded the Bel Canto Choirs and Orchestra and the St. Louis-area Cornerstone Chorale and Brass, renowned for their concerts around the country. Arvid Berg conducted an annual Christmas concert at Oak Grove Lutheran High School in Fargo; the school borrowed the center panels of Concordia's mural—all that would fit on their small stage—to replace their backdrop, lost in the 1997 flood. Certainly, there are others among the hundreds of Concordia choir alumni who have conducted church, high school and college choirs and community groups in programs echoing Concordia's Christmas Concerts.

On the practical side, the thousands who see the concerts each year have economic impact as well. The late Lloyd Sveen '40, an editor at *The Forum*, once surveyed local businessmen regarding the biggest drawing card to Fargo-Moorhead during the year. He was rather surprised to find most of them responded, "the Concordia Christmas Concerts."

For Concordia, the Christmas Concert has never been a "cash cow." In fact, in the early days, it put the college in the hole every year, until reserved seating not only helped pay for the event, but even contributed to funding other musical groups on campus. Still, the concert at best is a break-even event.

As such, it truly remains Concordia's "Christmas gift to the Midwest"—brightly wrapped and beautiful, part of a tradition, yet always a wonderful surprise.

"People always say it's the best yet," chuckled Gordon Moe. "You hear that every year: 'No, I'm serious this time. It was just great—the best ever.'"

Both Concordia's admissions office and the music department periodically published picture postcards featuring the Christmas Concerts.

Concordia's orchestra played the prelude and accompanied the choirs during the 1997 televised concert, adding dimension and color.

'A Gift from the House'

White-haired, gracious and unflappable, Mary Ann McDougall was longtime coordinator of Christmas Concert ticket sales. She always enjoyed chatting with the people she met. One conversation in particular "was especially warming to me," she wrote:

Mary Ann McDougall

During ticket sales, we have Christmas music playing in the background. A beautiful Viennese waltz was on—and at that moment a gentleman walked in the door to purchase a ticket. I mentioned the music and jokingly asked him to waltz with me. When he spoke, I noted an accent that seemed to be European. He told me his home was in Connecticut. I remarked he was dressed warmly for our cold weather, with a warm coat and wool scarf around his neck. He said they had been given to him, for he was a resident of a homeless shelter in Moorhead.

My heart was touched. I felt if this dear man wished to attend this concert, it should be a gift from the house. He thanked me kindly and went on his way.

As a sequel to this story, the man came back the following year and purchased four tickets, as he was taking his friends. He informed me he was now living in an apartment. How happy I was!

"Almighty God, you made this holy night shine with the brightness of the true light. Grant that here on earth we may walk in the light of Jesus' presence, and in the last day wake to the brightness of his glory."

—Closing Christmas Concert narration

Chapter 7

COMPLINE

The Legacy

In spite of the rate at which our society changes, people keep coming back. It must say something. And that's a big responsibility, because the Christmas Concerts are a living, breathing tradition. Someday someone will take over for you. Someday someone will take over for me. We have to plant good seeds, and we have to stick to what we believe. That's more than important; it's crucial.

—René Clausen to David Hetland

Faith traditions become our anchors. Over and over again, people who believe find themselves returning for sustenance – in times of sorrow, hope, fear or joy – to familiar Bible passages, the poetry of the Psalms and to the lyrical melodies of beloved hymns.

Another of those faith traditions is the festival season of Christmas – the celebration of God born as one among us, the fulfillment of promise and the renewal of hope. Concordia's Christmas Concerts, too, are a tradition that sustains tradition. And that, as René Clausen has said, is an important and joyful responsibility to bear.

For choir and ensemble members, participating in a Christmas Concert is unforgettable. After graduation, said Clausen, they all want to be back for this event whenever they can. It's a "many-threaded tradition," the conductor added, that becomes a part of them. Liv Rosin affirmed, "Once you've been in a Christmas Concert, you know what the other people are feeling and so, in a sense, even though you're not up there performing, you still feel included."

Ingrid Christiansen remembered how her father Paul once equated singing in the choir with building a house of worship:

> One spring, the inevitable time came for our final concert together. On graduation day as we lined up in the basement of the gym, waiting to march on and sing together for the last time, many of us were feeling an incredible sense of loss and sadness. . . . He said to us, "You have built a fine cathedral." Although we would soon sing our last notes together, that fact did not diminish the value of what we had done—the beauty of the cathedral we had built together.

At her father's memorial service, Ingrid said, "We make better music in our lives than we could have imagined possible. . . . He has truly built a fine cathedral."

TELLING THE STORY

Importantly, for Concordia College, the Christmas Concert reflects the college's mission. "It displays the exuberance of our people and our energy," said Paul Dovre. Added Peter Halverson, "There's nothing that speaks so loudly (of the college's mission) as does that concert."

Yet any public relations motivation remains only a secondary goal, said Dovre:

> Our primary goal is to tell the story. I don't think you want to fool with a good thing, and so there's every reason to avoid change.
> I do wish that we had a better national platform for the concert—this sort of occasional radio and television production is, I think, not adequate to its quality. We need a systematic way to get it shared around the country, to give it continuity from year to year.

All who participate—from singers, instrumentalists and narrators to painters and technical experts to ticket sellers and custodians—know they are part of something greater than themselves, a collaboration of

Clara Duea

Herman Monson

Paul Christiansen

Cyrus Running

gifts that is truly unique. This annual "Christmas gift to the Midwest" is one in which, as Erling Rolfsrud '36 wrote, "the individual contributions of hundreds of students and staff members lose themselves in the larger purpose of glorifying God."

Always, our challenge is to keep the Christmas Concert message firmly rooted in biblical teachings but to deliver it in a verbal and visual language that will be understood by all today. René Clausen describes it as keeping "one foot in the past and one foot in the future":

We are reinterpreting the same event with a newness and freshness, but still connected to the time-honored traditions. It was like that for Paul J.—the concert was never just the same. He was always writing new music, finding new composers. It's in the tradition for the Christmas Concerts to live and become new.

Simply put, we are retelling an ancient story. When I consider the role of each person involved in presenting these concerts and the energy we all expend, I am still mystified by the power of our combined effort. And I remain totally committed to my hope that the best

concert will be our next one. The story always remains the same but, as Paul Nesheim pointed out, "We have one of the most beautiful ways to tell it."

Occasionally, *how* that story is told seems to develop in amazing (and unplanned) ways. As creators of the Christmas Concert music and art, we're not always sure how that takes place. "There's something that happens in that concert that doesn't happen in any other," said orchestra conductor Bruce Houglum. "There's a spirit that reaches people at a different level. I think most of them are surprised that they are touched in unexpected ways.

"These concerts are God-honoring, and as a result of that, I think, God honors the performance."

AN AFFIRMING PROMISE

I've spoken with others about the tendency to sometimes take these concerts for granted. For months we prepare, and in 90 minutes, they're over. But their sights and sounds continue to echo and to sustain each of us throughout the year until we return next December. Perhaps, in retrospect, we have learned that wondrous things can take place in what Barbara (Aitken)

James Cermak

Bryan Duncan

René Clausen

David Hetland

People from every circumstance are comforted and encouraged by the Christmas Concert messsage.

Swanson '76 called "the saint-filled gym." Carrying a lighted candle in the concert recessional, she felt joy in God's gifts and in the possibilities she could envision for her life. Audience members, too, feel that presence and that blessing.

While there are bound to be some changes—witness the addition of full orchestra, the increasing complexity of the mural and technical developments in lighting—Clausen believes the essence of the Christmas Concerts will remain consistent:

I'm interested to see what technology is going to bring us. As long as it does not become a gadget, as long as it remains an artistic possibility that maintains the integrity of the concert— then we ought to look at it. There will always be new music, but we need to stay rooted in traditional literature.

People want to hear the word of God, and they want it interpreted for them in music and visual art. Our culture is searching for truth, and so, by the end of these concerts, our audience and our students can say, "This I believe."

What's the attraction of working on this project year after year?

For me, there are two answers, really, and both are selfish. I love being with this diverse group of people. Together we've discovered that spending so much time on our knees (painting blue dogs and purple camels) at that time of year is probably appropriate.

And the second answer is what I've seen so often at the Sunday afternoon concert. That's when wheelchairs occupy most of the front row, each bearing a person challenged by age or disability. There, for a brief moment, they seem to find relief from daily burdens and are affirmed with God's eternal promise of hope— here presented to each person through the word, the music and the art of Christmas.

For them, and for us all, the blessing of "Compline" echoes softly and richly:

The Lord almighty grant us a quiet night and peace at the last.
It is good to give thanks to the Lord, to sing praise to your name, O Most High;
to herald your love in the morning, your truth at the close of the day. Amen.

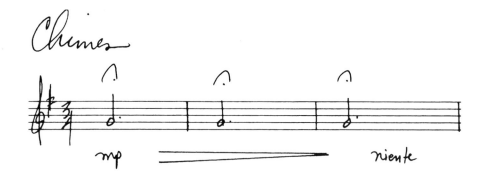

"You have built a fine cathedral."

—Paul J. Christiansen

Works by unattributed composers/arrangers or works performed by choirs, ensembles or audiences are indicated as "hymn" wherever possible. Many unattributed hymns were arranged by Paul J. Christiansen or René Clausen. Numbers following composer/arranger indicate year(s) performed.

Fum, Fum, Fum: *arr. Larry Fleming,*78; *Spanish carol,*55.

Geistliches Wiegenlied (spiritual Cradle Song): *Albert Kranz,*37, 43,46,84.

Gelobet sei der Herr: *German,*92.

Gesu Bambino: *Pietro A. Yon,*28, 31,32,33.

Gifts and Talents: *Paul J. Christiansen,*81.

Glad Tidings Bringing: *Polish carol, arr. Theron Kirk,*70.

Gladsome Radiance: *Alexander Gretchaninoff,*45.

Gloria,55; *Jeffrey Rickard,*96.

Gloria (from Twelfth Mass): *W.A. Mozart,*30,31,36.

Gloria (second movement): *John Rutter,*92.

Gloria Deus: *Brazilian,*92.

Gloria in Excelsis Deo: *Martin Shaw,*59.

Glorification: *F. Melius Christiansen,*68,87.

Glorious Things of Thee Are Spoken: *Franz Joseph Haydn,*76.

Glory Be to God: *Jean Berger,*68, 81,95; *Sergei Rachmaninoff,*38, 45,52,92; *Sergei Rachmaninoff, arr. Overby,*46; *recessional chant,*53.

Glory to God: *Alan Gibbs,*74.

Glory to God (from Messiah): *G.F. Handel,*29.

Glory to God in the Highest: *Randall Thompson,*60,63,66,79,97.

Glory to God in the Highest (from the Christmas Oratorio): *J.S. Bach,*60,62.

Go Tell It on the Mountain: *Christmas spiritual,*68,74,80,83; *arr. Carolyn Jennings,*88.

Go, Pretty Child: *Jack M. Jarrett,*97.

God Lives in You (Don't You Realize): *Paul J. Christiansen,*75.

God of Our Fathers: *George W. Warren,*85.

God Rest Ye Merry, Gentlemen: *English carol,*72,74,81,87; *arr. Roger Wagner,*84.

God So Loved the World: *Paul J. Christiansen,*77.

Good Christian Friends, Rejoice!: *hymn,*86,87,89.

Good Friends, Give Ear: *French Noel,*64.

Good King Wenceslas: *arr. Kevin McChesney (bells),* 98; *arr. David Townsend,*74,78,79,83,84,85,86.

Gracious Spirit: *Louis Gottschalk,*78.

Hacia Belén va un borrico (Toward Bethlehem We Go): *Spanish carol, arr. Robert Shaw-Alice Parker,*94,98.

Hail to the Brightness: *hymn,*66.

Hail to the Brightness of Zion's Glad Morning: *Lowell Mason,*66.

Hallelujah: *J.S. Bach,*36.

Hallelujah Chorus (from Messiah): *G.F. Handel,*28,71,78,91.

Hallelujah to the Lord: *F. Melius Christiansen,*37.

Hallelujah, Amen: *G.F. Handel,*46.

Hark! The Herald Angels Sing: *Felix Mendelssohn-William H. Cummings,*43,47,48,49,50,51, 53,54,66,68,71,74,75,77,80,83.

Hasten Swiftly, Hasten Softly: *Slovak carol, arr. Richard Kountz,*57,84.

Have No Fear, Little Flock: *Heinz Werner Zimmerman,*85.

Have Ye Not Known?: *Randall Thompson,*49,59.

He is Born: *arr. Roger Wagner,*83; *arr. Robert Wetzler,*88.

He is Born, the Divine Christ Child: *French,*75,76; *French carol, arr. Daniel Breedon,*94.

He Shall Feed His Flock: *G.F. Handel,*61,85.

Heiligstenacht: *Kranz,*38.

Here is the Little Door: *Herbert Howells,*90.

Here We Come a-Caroling: *English wassail song,*73.

Hodie: *Ralph Vaughan Williams, arr. René Clausen,*86.

Hodie Christus Natus Est (Christ is Born Today): *Benjamin Britten,*73,76; *Giovanni da Palestrina,*57,66; *Jan P. Sweelinck,*48,52; *Healey Willan,*48,49,54,65,90.

Holy is God: *C.P.E. Bach,*61.

Hosanna: *F. Melius Christiansen,*46; *Randall Thompson,*60.

Hosanna in the Highest: *Söderman,*45.

Hosianna (from Advent Motet): *Gustav Schreck,*32.

How Blest Are They: *Peter Ilich Tchaikowsky,*46.

How Far Is It to Bethlehem?: *English, arr. David Wilcox,*73; *traditional English children's carol,*50,84,92.

How Great Are Thy Wonders: *Georg Schumann,* 98.

How Great Our Joy!: *German carol, arr. John Rutter,*87,96.

How Lovely is Thy Dwelling Place: *Johannes Brahms,*80.

How Still He Rests (Lies): *Brent Pierce,*82,91,96.

How Unto Bethlehem: *carol,*77.

Hymn to the Virgin: *Benjamin Britten,*93.

I Am a Poor Wayfaring Stranger: *American,*79.

I Am the Vine, You Are the Branches: *Paul J. Christiansen,*77.

I Heard a Great Voice: *Paul J. Christiansen,*75.

I Lift Mine Eyes Unto the Hills: *René Clausen,*95.

I Praise Thee: *Kønig, arr. F. Melius Christiansen,*48.

I Sat Down Under His Shadow: *Edward Bairstow,*54.

I Saw Three Ships: *English carol,* 97; *English carol, arr. James Melby,*89,94.

I Sing of a Maiden: *Patrick Hadley,*97.

I Wonder as I Wander: *Appalachian carol, arr. John Jacob Niles,*60,68,74,83.

I Would Sing of Mary's Child: *Austin Lovelace,*65.

Ideo Gloria in Excelsis Deo: *David Kraehenbuehl,*60,75,92.

If By His Spirit: *J.S. Bach,*75.

In Dulci Jubilo: *arr. Anna Laura Page (bells),* 98.

In Heaven Above: *Norwegian folk song,*41.

In Jesus' Name: *Kingo, arr. Herman Monson,*27,28.

In Terra Pax: *Gerald Finzi,*93.

In the Beginning: *René Clausen,*89.

In the Bleak Midwinter: *arr. Karen Buckwalter (bells),*96; *Harold Darke,*97; *hymn,*88.

In the Shadow of Your Wings: *Claude-Michel D'Étoile*,*95.

Infant Holy, Infant Lowly: *Polish carol,*73,88; *Polish carol, arr. Paul J. Christiansen,*94,98.

Is a Light Shining in the Heavens: *spiritual,*82.

It Came Upon the Midnight Clear: *hymn,*45,46,76,77,79, 85; *arr. Arnold Sherman (bells),* 98; *Richard S. Willis,*43,72,82.

Jeg Er Saa Glad (How Glad I Am Each Christmas Eve): *arr. Hokanson,*66; *arr. Peder Knudsen,* 78; *Norse folk song,*48,49,57,59, 64,60,71,74,76,79,82,83,87, 91,94.

Jerusalem: *Darius Milhaud,*60.

Jesu Fili, Virginis, Miserere Nobis: *Donald Prindle,*38.

Jesu, Priceless Treasure (three movements): *J.S. Bach,*34.

Jesu, As Thou Art Our Savior: *Benjamin Britten,*49,58,78.

Jesu, Joy of Man's Desiring: *arr. Daniel Breedon,*88.

Jesulein: *Francis F. Hagen,*77.

Jesus Christ, the Apple Tree: *Elizabeth Poston,*97.

Jesus Only: *Rotoli,*33.

Jesus, Rest Your Head: *Black American spiritual,*68.

Jesus Was Born On This Day: *English carol,*50.

Jesus, Jesus, Rest Your Head: *Appalachian folk song, arr. Murrae Freng,*84.

Joseph and the Angel: *Virgil Thompson,*54.

Joseph Dearest, Joseph Mine (Joseph Lieber, Joseph Mein): *Albert Kranz,*58; *traditional German,*62,72,85.

Joy: *F. Melius Christiansen,*42.

Joy to the World: *American carol (G.F. Handel),*27,36,37,41,42, 44,45,47,50,51,52,54,55,61, 62,63,64,68,71,73,77,82,84, 85; *arr. Charles Forsberg,*86,89, 96,97; *arr. Lowell Mason,*78,79; *arr. Mary Kay Parrish (bells),*96.

Joyful, Joyful We Adore Thee (Sing of Joy): *hymn, Ludwig van Beethoven,*77,88,95.

Joyous Christmas Song: *F.A. Gevaert,*65.

Keeping Holy Vigil: *German traditional,*56.

King David (Finale): *Arthur Honegger,*93.

Kyrie Eleison: *plain song,*64.

Larghetto: *G.F. Handel,*40.

Largo from Concerto in C Major: *Ludwig van Beethoven,*34.

Laudamus Te (We Praise Thee): *René Clausen,*94; *Francis Poulenc,*91.

Lay Down Your Staffs: *French carol,*61.

Lead On, O King Eternal: *Henry T. Smart,*82,85.

Let All Men Sing God's Praises: *hymn,*46.

Let All Mortal Flesh Keep Silence: *French carol,*43,51.

Let All the Nations: *Volkmar Leisring,*57.

Let All the World in Every Corner Sing! *René Clausen,*95.

Let All Things Now Living: *Welsh tune, arr. René Clausen,*87,93.

Let the Whole Creation Cry: *hymn,*89.

Let Thy Blessed Spirit: *Paul Tschesnokoff,*38.

Lift High the Cross: *Sydney H. Nicholson, arr. Paul J. Christiansen,*84.

Lift Up Your Heads: *Gunnar Wennerberg,*27.

Lift Up Your Heads, Ye Mighty Gates: *Ralph Vaughan Williams-Olaf C. Christiansen,*70,77,84.

Jesus Only: *Rotoli,*33. —

Light Everlasting: *Olaf C. Christiansen,*82,91.

Little Star of Bethlehem (A Christmas Carol): *Charles Ives,*80.

Lo! To Us is Born an Infant: *Liebhold,*40,50,53.

Lo, How a Rose e'er Blooming: *German hymn, Michael Praetorius,*39,56,58,65,86,87,88, 91,93,95; *arr. Gregg Temple,*72.

Lo, I Reveal Unto Thee: *Gallus,*55.

Lord Cause Thy Face to Shine: *Costa,*33.

Lord, Thou Hast Been Our Refuge: *Ralph Vaughan Williams,*88.

Lost in the Night: *F. Melius Christiansen,*89,95.

Love Came Down at Christmas: *carol,*88.

Love Divine, All Love Excelling: *John Zundel,*79.

Love One Another: *Paul J. Christiansen,*80.

Lullaby: *Gerhardt Schroth,*57.

Lullaby on Christmas Eve: *F. Melius Christiansen,*38,45,55, 63,66,87,91.

Lullay: *carol,*77.

Lully, Lulla, Thou Little Tiny Child: *Kenneth Leighton,*89.

Lute Book Lullaby: *George Oldroyd,*52.

Lux Aeterna: *John Rutter,*87,93.

Magnificat: *J.S. Bach,*92; *Daniel Moe,*94.

Make Us One: *arr. Paul J. Christiansen,*82.

March of the Kings: *provincial,*75.

Mary Had a Baby: *spiritual,*75,80.

Mary Sat Spinning: *German (Wendish) folk tune,*56,58,62,83.

Mary's Response (Magnificat): *arr. Paul J. Christiansen,*53,78.

Mary's Wonder: *John Seagard,*87.

Masters in This Hall: *English carol,*76; *English (bells),*97.

Meditation from Christ, The Light of Life, Op. 29: *Edward Elgar,*97.

Meet and Right It Is: *Kalinnikoff,*43; *P. Turchaninoff,*44.

Messiah (excerpts): *G.F. Handel,*37.

Me-Thought I Heard a Maiden Sing: *Donald Prindle,*52.

Mexican Christmas Procession: *Mexican folk tune,*59,71,81.

Mine Eyes Have Seen the Glory of the Coming of the Lord: *William Steff,*74.

Mother's Cradle Song: *F. Melius Christiansen,*42.

Mothering God, You Gave Me Birth: *Carolyn Jennings,*96.

Music for Flute and Strings: *J.S. Bach,*46.

My Dancing Day: *arr. Robert Shaw-Alice Parker,*93.

My God, How Wonderful Thou Art: *Scotch Psalter,*79.

My Shepherd Will Supply My Need: *arr. Virgil Thompson,*54.

My Song In the Night: *Southern folk melody, arr. Paul J. Christiansen,*67,94.

Negro Bell Carol: *Willis L. James,*64,85.

Noel: *Koch,*64.

Noël Ayisyen: *Emile Desamours,*95.

Noel Nouvelet: *French,*75.

Now Found is the Fairest of Roses: *traditional,*62.

Now Sing We, Now Rejoice: *German hymn,*41,43,45,76.

Now Thank We All Our God: *Cornelius,*39.

Now the Feast: *Marty Haugen,*96.

Now the Silence: *Carl Schalk,*96.

Nunc Dimittis: *Alexander Gretchaninoff,*34.

Nunc Dimittis: *Robert Scholz,*96.

O Be Joyful: *Bohemian,*71,84.

O Beautiful Yuletide: *F. Melius Christiansen,*69.

O Bread of Life From Heaven: *Isaac,*72.

O Brother Man: *Alfred Scott-Gatty,*73.

O Christ, Our True and Only Light: *German,*66,72,82.

O Clap Your Hands: *Ralph Vaughan Williams,*71.

O Come, All Ye Children: *Johann Schulz,*81.

O Come, All Ye Faithful: *arr. G. Winston Cassler,*79,81; *arr. René Clausen,*91; *hymn,*42,43,46,48, 49,50,51,55,60,62,64,76; *arr. Shover- René Clausen,*86; *John F. Wade,*75,78.

O Come, Let Us Sing a New Song of Salvation Unto the Lord: *Paul J. Christiansen,*80.

O Come, Let Us Sing a New Song (Unto the Lord): *80.

O Come, Little Children: *German carol,*93; *traditional German carol, arr. David Childs,*92.

O Come, O Come, Emmanuel: *traditional/Gregorian melody,* 48,58,68,78,89.

O Darkest Woe: *chorale,*64,73.

O Day Full of Grace: *Christoph Weyse, arr. F. Melius Christiansen,* 49,54,62,72,81,83.

O Fillii et Filliae (Ye Sons and Daughters of the King): *Volkmar Leisring,*51.

Today is Born Emmanuel: *Michael Praetorius,*58.

Today, Heaven Sings: *Kenneth Jennings,*97.

Tomorrow Shall Be My Dancing Day: *John Gardner,*91; *John Rutter,*86,88,98.

Torches: *Gallican,*91.

Tree of Life: *Marty Haugen,*97.

'Twas in the Moon of Winter time: *hymn,*98; *arr. Kevin McChesney (bells),*98.

Twelfth Night: *Samuel Barber,*92.

Tyrle, Tyrlow, Tyrle, Tyrlow (Tyrley, Tyrlow): *Healey Willan,*66; *Peter Warlock,*89.

Ukrainian Bell Carol: *arr. Hart Morris (bells),*96,98.

Unto Us a Child is Born: *Geoffrey Shaw,*73.

Verbum caro factum est: *Hans Leo Hassler,*87.

Vigil: *F. Melius Christiansen,*42,47,73.

Villancio: *Puerto Rican carol, arr. Gail Downey (bells),*97.

Vision of Peace: *Jean Berger,*63.

Wake, Awake For Night is Flying: *Philipp Nicolai, arr. F. Melius Christiansen,*41,46,48, 53,58,92,96; *Philipp Nicolai, arr. Kathrine Jordahl Larson (bells),*97.

Waltz in A Major: *Brahms,*33.

We Hasten, O Master: *J.S. Bach,*88.

We Praise Thee: *Kastalsky,*43,44.

We Three Kings: *John H. Hopkins, Jr., arr. Arnold Sherman (bells),*96.

We'll Dress the House: *Alfred Burt,*73.

We've Been (A While) A'Wandering: *Yorkshire carol, arr. Olaf C. Christiansen,*54,59,84.

Welcome: *F. Melius Christiansen,*53.

What Child is This: *arr. Paul J. Christiansen,*62; *English carol,* 75,76,80,83,86; *arr. Gregg Temple,*72.

What Shall I Bring: *arr. Lloyd and Debbie Pfautsch,*75.

What Sweeter Music: *R.R. Bennett,*94.

When at Creation's Dawn There Was No Sound: *James Clemens,*98.

When Christmas Morn is Dawning: *German folk tune,* 58,68,69,71,72,74,76,82,84,93; *arr. Katherine Jordahl Larson (bells),*96.

While By My Sheep I Watched at Night: *German carol,*80.

While By Our (Their) Sleeping Flocks We (They) Lay: *17th century German carol,*48,55.

While Mary Rocks Her Child to Rest: *Slovak carol,*68.

While Stars Their Vigil Keep: *Morten Luvaas,*57,67,83,95.

Will Thy Spirit Uphold Me: *Johannes Brahms,*78.

Winds Through the Olive Trees: *American folk hymn, arr. Paul J. Christiansen,*72,78,93.

Winter Passes Over: *Richard Purvis,*51.

With Joy We Depart (from O Day Full of Grace): *F. Melius Christiansen,*69.

Wolcum Yole! (from A Ceremony of Carols): *Benjamin Britten,* 54,80.

Wondrous Love: *Southern folk melody,*65.

Ya viene la vieja: *arr. Shaw-Parker,*84.

Ye Lands to the Lord: *hymn,*85.

Ye Servants of God: *Michael Haydn,*83; *William Havergal,*83.

Ye Shall Have a Song: *Randall Thompson,*48,49,59.

Ye Sons and Daughters of the King: *Volkmar Leisring,*64,86.

Ye Watchers and Ye Holy Ones: *traditional,*63.

Yuletide: *F. Melius Christiansen,*41.

Zion, Praise Thy Savior: *Dietrich Buxtehude,*49.

* *pseudonym for René Clausen*

Concordia Christmas Concert Music Recordings

Let Heaven And Nature Sing 1997

1. Meditation from Lux Christi, *Edward Elgar* 2. Tree Of Life, *Marty Haugen (arr. René Clausen)* 3. Fantasia On Christmas Carols, *Ralph Vaughan Williams* 4. All Creatures Of Our God And King, *Traditional (arr. René Clausen)* 5. This Is My Father's World, *Franklin Sheppard (arr. Charles Forsberg)* 6. O Magnum Mysterium, *Morten Lauridsen* 7. I Sing Of A Maiden, *Patrick Hadley* 8. There Is No Rose, *Joel Martinson* 9. In The Bleak Midwinter, *Harold Darke* 10. A Lute Caroll, *Mary Elizabeth Caldwell* 11. Go, Pretty Child, *Jack M. Jarrett* 12. Christmas Fanfare, *Cardon Burnham* 13. Today, Heaven Sings, *Kenneth Jennings* 14. Angels Carol, *John Rutter* 15. Glory To God In The Highest, *Randall Thompson* 16. O Little Town Of Bethlehem, *Traditional (arr. Ralph Vaughan Williams)* 17. Past Three A Clock, *Traditional (arr. Charles Wood)* 18. Masters In This Hall, *Traditional (arr. Arnold B. Sherman)* 19. Coventry Carol, *Traditional(arr. Paul Nesheim)* 20. I Saw Three Ships, *Traditional (arr. David Willcocks)* 21. Sir Christémas, *William Mathias* 22. The Three Kings, *Healey Willan* 23. Psalm 150, *René Clausen*

Light Everlasting 1991

1. Prelude On Sent Forth, *J. Robert Hanson* 2. O Come, All Ye Faithful, *Traditional (arr. Blaine Shover & René Clausen)* 3. Laudamus te, *Francis Poulenc* 4. Light Everlasting, *Olaf C. Christiansen* 5. There Is No Rose, *Benjamin Britten* 6. Silent Night, *Franz Gruberr (arr. René Clausen)* 7. A Spotless Rose, *Herbert Howells* 8. Sanctus, *John Rutter* 9. This Little Babe, *Benjamin Britten* 10. Salvation Is Created, *P. Tschesnokoff* 11. Hallelujah, *George F. Handel* 12. Sent Forth By God's Blessing, *arr. René Clausen*

For Unto Us A Child Is Born 1990

1. Campanae parisienes, *Ottorino Resphighi* 2. Let All Mortal Flesh, *arr. René Clausen* 3. Agnus Dei (from Requiem), *John Rutter* 4. O, How Shall I Receive Thee, *Gustav Schreck (arr. Olaf C. Christiansen)* 5. For Unto Us A Child Is Born, *George F. Handel* 6. Resonet In Laudibus, *Z. Randall Strooge* 7. The Christmas Symbol, *F. Melius Christiansen* 8. A La Nanita Nana, *arr. Norman Luboff* 9. Estampie Natalis, *Vaclav Nelhybel* 10. Sanctus from Requiem, *Maurice Duruflé* 11. Pat-a-Pan, *Clare Grundman* 12. Carol of the Drum, *Czech Carol (arr. Katherine K. Davis)* 13. Closing, *arr. René Clausen*

Prepare Ye 1974

1. Chimes 2. Introduction 3. Recitative - Prepare Ye The Way Of The Lord 4. Interlude 5. Interlude—Prepare ye 6. The Annunciation 7. Mary's Response (Magnificat) 8. Processional 9. Prepare Ye 10. O Holy Night, *Adolph Adam* 11. Deck The Halls 12. God Rest Ye Merry Gentlemen 13. Simple Gifts 14. Jeg Er Saa Glad 15. Interlude 16. Processional— Prepare Ye 17. This Is Our God 18. Recessional 19. Mine Eyes Have See The Glory Of The Coming Of The Lord, *William Steff* 20. Recitative 21. Interlude 22. Prepare Ye, Get Ready 23. Go Tell It On The Mountain, *Spiritual* 24. Chimes

King of Kings 1971

1. Chimes 2. Introduction 3. The Desert Shall Blossom As A Rose, *Paul J. Christiansen* 4. Interlude 5. Processional 6. Clap Your Hands All People, *F. Melius Christiansen* 7. O Clap Your Hands, *Ralph Vaughn Williams* 8. Processional—Thy Kingdom Come, *F. Melius Christiansen* 9. When Christmas Morn Is Dawning, *German folk song* 10. Angels Hovered Round, *French carol* 11. This Little Light Of Mine, *Spiritual* 12. A Christmas Carol, *Zoltan Kodaly* 13. Hymn for Audience—Joy To The World 14. Hymn for Audience—The First Noel 14. Christmas Carols Sung By Choirs 15. The Happy Christmas Comes Once More, *Norwegian* 16. O How Beautiful The Sky, *Danish* 17. Mexican Christmas Procession, *Mexican* 18. O Be Joyful, *Bohemian* 19. Jeg Er Saa Glad, *Norwegian* 20. Hymn for Audience, Hark The Herald Angels Sing 21. Hymn for Audience, They Little Ones, Dear Lord, Are We, *Schulz* 22. Song Of Mary, *(Spanish) Christiansen-Kranz* 23. Silent Night 24. Interlude 25. Recitative 26. Interlude 27. The Prayer Of Saint Francis Of Asissi 28. Interlude 29. The King Of Love My Shepherd Is, *Irish tune* 30. Interlude 31. Pontius Pilate, *Paul Christiansen* 32. Interlude 33. Hallelujah Chorus, *Handel* 34. Recessional 35. The King Of Love My Shepherd Is, *Irish tune* 36. King Of Kings, And Lord Of Lords 37. Chimes

Concordia Choir The New Jerusalem and The Christmas Story (CDLP-5) 1955

1. Chimes 2. Introduction 3. Interlude 4. The Morning Star Upon Us Gleams 5. The Sleep Of The Child Jesus, *Gevaert* 6. Angels We Have Heard On High, *French carol* 7. Lullaby On Christmas Eve, *F. Melius Christiansen* 8. Silent Night 9. Chimes

Concordia Choir Album (CDLP-2) 1950

1. Be Not Afraid, *Johann Sebastian Bach* 2. An Apostrophe To The Heavenly Hosts, *Healey Willan* 3. Vinea Mea Electa, *Francis Poulenc* 4. Thy Little Ones, Dear Lord, Are We, *arr. John Dahle* 5. How Far Is It To Bethlehem, *Traditional (arr. Paul Christiansen)* 6. The Three Kings, *Catalonian Nativity song* 7. Jesus Was Born On This Day, *English folk carol (arr. Paul Christiansen)* 8. Away In A Manger, *Traditional* 9. A Flemish Carol, *arr. Paul Christiansen* 10. The Cradle, *Austrian Nativity Song (arr. Paul Christiansen)* 11. Jeg Er Saa Glad, *arr. Margrethe Hokanson* 12. Silent Night, Holy Night, *Traditional*

Around the Christmas Tree circa 1950

1. Silent Night, Holy Night, *Traditional* 2. How Far Is It To Bethlehem?, *English Traditional (arr. Paul Christiansen)* 3. The Three Kings, *Catalonian Nativity song* 4. Jesus Was Born On This Day, *English folk carol (arr. Paul Christiansen)* 5. Away In A Manger, *Traditional* 6. A Flemish Carol, *arr. Paul Christiansen* 7. The Cradle, *Austrian Nativity song (arr. Paul Christiansen)* 8. Jeg Er Saa Glad, *arr. Margrethe Hokanson* 9. Thy Little Ones, Dear Lord, Are We, *arr. John Dahle* 10. Be Not Afraid, *Johann Sebastian Bach*

Boldfaced numbers indicate references to photographs or illustrations

ACKNOWLEDGMENTS

A book of this complexity can never be the product of a single author. Rather, it is the interest, talent and commitment of many that make possible a compilation such as this one. I am especially grateful to Gordon Moe and Paul Dovre who shared my vision and dared make it happen and to Eleanor Christiansen, Sharon Hoverson, Jaci Lima and John Borge who made it happen better. To those listed elsewhere, your priceless contributions of stories and "stuff" helped breathe life into this monster.

Special thanks must go to my manuscript readers for their sensitivities and attention to detail: Jim Cermak, Eleanor Christiansen, Michael Culloton, Paul Dovre, Jerilyn Forde, Mary Hetland, Sharon Hoverson, Gordon Moe, Louise Nettleton, Carolyn Osborne and Thomas Thomsen. Eleanor passed away in July 1999, shortly before final publication of this book. Her contributions were invaluable.

To each member of the Hetland Ltd. staff who worked directly or indirectly on this book, it would be an understatement to say that it could not have happened without you. I am especially grateful to Doug Fliss for his skillful and precise graphic design skills and to Karen Stensrud for her invaluable contributions to both the editorial content and the pre-press production process. This was a joyful effort because we worked so well together.

Then, there were the following people who so generously responded to my inquiries for materials and, in some cases, consented to personal interviews:

Don Aasland, Paul Allen, Lowell Almen, Alden Anderson, Edward Anderson, Robert Anderson, Ron and Linda Anderson, Carl and June Bailey, Charles Beck, Donald Bentley, Carlin Berg, Eileen (Ackerson) Blixrud, John Borge, Lori Borgeson, Dean Bowman, May Bredeson, Phyllis Bryn-Julson, Kathy Buck, Norma Buxton, John Carlander, Ann Cease, James Cermak, Tom Christenson, Eleanor Christiansen, Erik Christiansen, Ingrid Christiansen, Karl Christiansen, René Clausen, Rachel L. DeBoer, Les Dehlin, Beth Dille, Paul and Mardeth Dovre, Bryan Duncan, Ione Eckre, Carroll Engelhardt, Heidi Marie (Rust) Erdahl, Erling Erickson, Jerilyn Forde, Larry Fleming, The Forum, Mary Galbreath, Larry Gedde, Donald Geiken, Sonia Gisvold, Mark Halaas, Rusty and Mary Helen Halaas, Andrea Halgrimson, G. Howard Hall, H. Chris Hallanger, Peter Halverson, J. Robert and Lois Hanson, Paul Hanson, Michelle Hayes, Marlys Herring, Rachel Hiebert, Janet (Klemmer) Hoberg, Caren Holm-Martin, Bruce Houglum, Sharon and Bill Hoverson, Pam (Haugstul) Humphrey, A. Bruce Jacobs, Bob Johnson, Cecil Johnson, Jean Johnson, Myrna Johnson, Casey and Loraine Jones, Dale Lammi, David Langseth, Arthur Larson, David Larson, Lowell Larson, Sylvia Larson, Carl Lee, Ellen Liddle, Helene Lind, Kathy (Romsdahl) Lindquist, Robert Loeffler, Meggan Manlove, Karl Maurer, Esther McDermid, Mary Ann McDougall, Ray Melheim, Mary Melroe, Karla Mickelson, Gordon Moe, Laura Moenke, Jane (Svingen) Mooberry, Herb Morgenthaler, Fred Nelson, Laura Nelson, Paul Nesheim, Louise Nettleton, Dorothy Olsen, Darlene (Gronseth) Olson, Jon Pederson, Joan Flewell Pennock, Crystal (Olson) Peterson, John Pierce, Alice Polikowski, Dennis Raymond, Jim Revier, Beth Ronning, Tim Running, Anne Running, Thorpe Running, Steve Schaefer, Janet (Skjonsby) Schennum, Vicki Vogel Schmidt, John Schultz, Liza Simpson, Vilgard (Daehlin) Sorgen, Helen (Hallanger) Stensrud, Karen Stensrud, Betty Strand, Ruth (Carlson) Summerside, Karin Svare, Barbara (Aitken) Swanson, Ann (Schroeder) Taylor, Jeanie Tennefos, Philip Thompson, Tim Tommerson, Peter Trier, Laree (McNeal) Trollinger, Jodi (Zabel) Van Rhee, Wayne Wagstrom, Mildred (Knudsvig) Wermager.

Photo and Illustration Credits

Front cover: **John Borge/Concordia College Photo Lab** (M, BC, BR); **Concordia Archives** (BL). ***Back Cover:*** **John Borge/Concordia College Photo Lab.** **Paul Allen:** 76TR; **Laura Buhr:** 81MR; **Carl Bailey:** 81BR; **Jon Bartelt:** 78R; **John Borge/Concordia College Photo Lab:** 3, 5, 27L, 34R, 42TR, 42B, 50B, 52R, 54B, 56R, 58R, 59BR, 61TL, 63L, 63BR, 66BL, 71L, 73BR, 76BR, 77L, 80TL, 86M, 90LC, 90-91B, 93TC, 93BR, 94BL, 96BL, 96R, 97BL, 97BR, 101TR, 103T, 105BR, 106BC, 108TL, 108TC, 109, 110TR, 111R, 112TL, 112LC, 112BL, 115RC, 115BR, 116, 118R, 119BL, 119LC, 119RC, 119BR, 121M, 128, inside back flap; **Dean Bowman:** 51BR, 85CC; **James Cermak:** 75BR; **Eleanor Christiansen:** 2, 21B, 26B, 39L, 41B, 45B, 46C, 47B, 77BR; **René and Frankie Clausen:** 1, 57BR, 58B, 120B; **Concordia College Archives:** 8, 12L, 13R, 16R, 17R, 20R, 22TR, 22B, 23L, 24R, 28B, 29BR, 34M, 34C, 36BR, 38B, 40BL, 41TL, 42LC, 44BL, 44R, 48R, 49BR, 49B, 50TC, 53B, 55BR, 56BL, 67L, 69L, 72R, 73BL, 75C, 76LC, 89L, 100L, 102BL, 102R, 112R, 115L, 118RC; **Concordia College Music Department:** 57L; **Concordia College Office of Communications:** 28R, 29L, 105TR, 119CL, 101L; **The Cobber:** 13L, 14L, 14R, 17L, 21L, 34L, 66B, 68R, 73TL, 88R, 118BLC, 120; **The Concordian:** 10L, 10R, 15; **Karin Denison:** 51L; **Art Hanson:** 85L; **Beth (Hopeman) Dille:** 38C, 121C; **H. Chris Hallanger:** 3, 11, 12R, 118L; **Hetland Ltd.:** 3, 4, 16TL, 18, 20TL, 21TR, 22,TL, 23TR, 24TL, 25TR, 26TL, 26R, 27TR, 28 TL, 29TR, 30L, 32TL, 33, 36TL, 37TR, 38TL, 39TR, 40TL, 41TR, 42TL, 43TR, 44TL, 45TR, 46TL, 47TR, 48TL, 49TR, 50TL, 51TR, 52TL, 53TL, 54TL, 55TR, 56TL, 57TR, 58TL, 58R, 59TR, 59BL, 60TL, 60BL, 61TR, 62, 63TR, 64, 66L, 67R, 68L, 69R, 70TL, 70BL, 70BC, 70BR, 71R, 72L, 73R, 74L, 74LL, 76L, 77R, 78BL, 78BR, 79L, 79TR, 79BR, 80BL, 80R, 81TL, 81ML, 81BL, 81TR, 82TL, 82BL, 82BR, 83L, 83R, 84TL, 84T, 84L, 85TC, 85BC, 85R, 86 insets, 88L, 89TR, 89BR, 90TL, 91TL, 90LC, 91R, 91TR, 91MR, 91BR, 92L, 92R, 93TR, 93L, 94TL, 94LC, 95TR, 95BR, 96TL, 97TL, 97TR, 98, 101BR, 102TL, 103BL, 105L, 106TL, 106BL, 106R, 107, 108B, 110B, 111TL, 111BL, 114C, 115TR; **Rachel Hiebert:** 14M; **Bruce Jacobs:** 94-95M; **Alfred Jesness:** 6; **Loraine Jones:** 114TL; **Ron Lee:** 68BL; **C. Robert Lewis:** 3, 113T, 113B; **Paul Nesheim:** 40R; **Cyrus and Eldrid Running Estate:** 23C, 47L, 74R, 75TR; **McCarty Studio:** 110L; ***Minneapolis Star and Tribune:*** 104; ***Moorhead Daily News:*** 20BL; ***Red River Scene:*** 55L; **St. Olaf College:** 36TR; **David Samson, Davon Press:** 31C; **Karen Stensrud:** 100R; **Tim Tommerson:** 94R, 95L, 95C; **Susan Vitalis:** 3, 31L; **Wayne Wagstrom:** 43L, 46R; **Warner Brothers Publications U.S., Inc.:** 25L.

Abbreviations used to designate picture positions on page:
M—Main	B—Bottom	L—Left
T—Top	C—Center	R—Right

from Seaming the Unseemly

. . . *Fragmented, disjointed,*
unseamed
pieces of a larger plan
seen only in a mind's eye.

Merging,
coming together,
the unseemly;
color meets color,
colliding,
then softly melting together.

Line meets line,
knitting together to create order out of chaos.
Water meets water,
uniting into a common stream.
Fish tumble in the waves.
Bubbles rise and
explode with playful delight.

. . . *Birds sweep across the spangled heavens.*
Angel wings flutter,
creating soft gentle winds that caress the blowing
trees on the distant hillside.
Gardens of mystery bloom abundantly,
embracing the Tree of Life and
framing its goodness.

. . . *Stars peek through the trees*
in curious wonderment.
Giraffes stretch their necks a little taller.
Fish jump a little higher.
Rays from the sun's day burn more brightly,
setting off the City of God never more golden!
Human forms begin leaping, twirling,
sister, brother
on their sacred journey to the New . . . .

—Vicki Vogel Schmidt, 1995

Vicki Schmidt's poem was inspired by the 1995 Christmas Concert.